T0196852

Cambridge Elements ≡

Elements in Publishing and Book Culture
edited by
Samantha Rayner
University College London
and
Rebecca Lyons
University of Bristol

CONTINGENT CANONS

African Literature and the Politics of Location

Madhu Krishnan

University of Bristol

CAMBRIDGE
UNIVERSITY PRESS

CAMBRIDGE
UNIVERSITY PRESS

University Printing House, Cambridge CB2 8BS, United Kingdom

One Liberty Plaza, 20th Floor, New York, NY 10006, USA

477 Williamstown Road, Port Melbourne, VIC 3207, Australia

314–321, 3rd Floor, Plot 3, Splendor Forum, Jasola District Centre,
New Delhi – 110025, India

79 Anson Road, #06–04/06, Singapore 079906

Cambridge University Press is part of the University of Cambridge.

It furthers the University's mission by disseminating knowledge in the pursuit of
education, learning, and research at the highest international levels of excellence.

www.cambridge.org
Information on this title: www.cambridge.org/9781108445375
DOI: 10.1017/9781108641920

First published 2019

A catalogue record for this publication is available from the British Library.

ISBN 978-1-108-44537-5 Paperback
ISSN 2514-8524 (online)
ISSN 2514-8516 (print)

Cambridge Elements

Contingent Canons

African Literature and the Politics of Location

Elements in Publishing and Book Culture

DOI: 10.1017/9781108641920
First published online: October 2018

Madhu Krishnan
University of Bristol

ABSTRACT: This study explores the mechanisms through which 'African literature', as a market category, has been consecrated within the global literary field. Drawing on archival, textual, and field-based research, it proposes that the normative story of African literary writing has functioned to efface a broader material history of African literary production located on and oriented to the continent itself.

KEYWORDS: African literature, book history, canonisation

ISBNs: 9781108445375 (PB), 9781108641920 (OC)
ISSNs: 2514–8516 (online), 2514–8524 (print)

Contents

Introduction

On 24 October 1968, Ngũgĩ wa Thiong'o, Henry Owuor-Anyumba, and Taban Lo Liyong presented a paper to the Department of English at the University of Nairobi, entitled 'On the Abolition of the English Department'. In this piece, the three men argue for the dissolution of the Department of English and its replacement with a Department of African Literature and Languages, contending that:

> This is not a change of names only. We want to establish the centrality of Africa in the department. This, we have argued, is justifiable on various grounds, the most important one being that education is a means of knowledge about ourselves. Therefore, after we have examined ourselves, we radiate outwards and discover peoples and worlds around us. With Africa at the centre of things, not existing as an appendix or a satellite of other countries and literatures, things must be seen from the African perspective.[1]

The arguments presented by Ngũgĩ and his colleagues touch upon many of the central issues which drive the processes of canonisation and literary consecration: the role of institutions as gatekeepers and mediators of value; the variety of relations which shape the literary field as a whole; the perceived connections and chasms across forms, genre, and media; and more. I would like to set Ngũgĩ's comment alongside another, seemingly

---

[1] Ngũgĩ wa Thiong'o, 'On the Abolition of the English Department', in *The Postcolonial Studies Reader*, first edition ed. by Bill Ashcroft, Gareth Griffiths, and Helen Tiffin (New York: Routledge, 1995), pp. 438–42 (p. 441).

disparate, moment from recent history. On 9 July 2011, the Republic of South Sudan was officially declared an independent state, recognised as such by Sudan (the state with whom the new republic had spent the previous decade embroiled in a protracted civil war), the United Nations, and the international community at large. Strangely, for a relatively small, land-locked African nation, the recognition of South Sudan as an independent republic made world headlines, occupying column inches and numerous analyses. What might at first seem a somewhat strange fixation, however, becomes all the more remarkable when placed in its historical context; for the independence of South Sudan marked only the second time that an African state would be declared independent not from a European coloniser but from another African state of which it was once a constituent part (the other example being Eritrea, which gained its independence from Ethiopia in 1993). What is remarkable here is that this was ever able to happen; the African Union is committed to upholding the integrity of territorial barriers as they stood at the time of independence from European colonisers, a stance which has sometimes exacerbated protracted independence and sectarian struggles (for instance, in Nigeria, the Democratic Republic of Congo, formerly Zaire, and Morocco). Set in this context South Sudan's declaration of independence – and the international community's recognition of that independence – marked the first time in decades in which the map of the African continent would depart from the futures decided for it in Berlin in 1884 when the competing imperial powers carved the continent up among themselves to share out its spoils.

What do these two moments have to do with publishing African literature? Quite a lot, I contend; my argument in this Element is that we cannot think about the contours of African literature as a global market category without considering its implication within the larger history through which the continent has come to function both as a physical space and a signifier in the world. At its heart, this is a history predicated on the fight over positions, positionings, and position-takings: how Africa and its literature is located in a global topography; the tension over who gets to decide that placement; and the struggles – internal and external – that mediate these processes. In *The Field of Cultural Production*, Pierre Bourdieu writes:

> The space of literary or artistic position-takings, i.e. the struc-
> tured set of the manifestations of the social agents involved in
> the field – literary or artistic works, of course, but also political
> acts of pronouncements, manifestos or polemics, etc. – is inse-
> parable from the space of literary or artistic positions defined by
> possession of a determinate quantity of specific capital (recogni-
> tion) and, at the same time, by occupation of a determinate
> position in the structure of the distribution of this specific
> capital. The literary or artistic field is a field of forces, but it is
> also a field of struggles tending to transform or conserve this
> field of forces.[2]

For Bourdieu, position-takings – and indeed the delineation of artistic positions – occur through the relational interaction of a wide variety of actors and
institutions who together ultimately define the contours of the literary field
through a continual and iterative process of competition over the various, finite
forms of capital available. With this vision of the literary field in mind, the body
of work that we conceive of as being African literature, too, emerges through
its relational position within an asymmetrically loaded field of cultural production and value, with correlations and crossovers with the larger discursive

---

[2] Pierre Boudieu, *The Field of Cultural Production* (Cambridge: Polity Press, 1993), p. 30.

matrices through which Africa comes into being in the world. Here, it is worth recalling James English, who observes that 'every form of "capital" everywhere exists not only in relation to one particular field, but in varying relations to all other fields and all other types of capital'.[3] In context of African literature, we might see these relations emerging in, for instance, the tendency to privilege those texts deemed to have sociological value, or the tendency to privilege certain forms and genres, particularly the novel. From early modes of reading which assimilated African literature into the larger anthropological discourse around the continent; to the overdetermined paradigm of writing back; to repeated debates about poverty porn and representation; to contemporary trends which focus on migrancy, diaspora, and the murky notion of Afropolitanism, African literature has been defined by a series of uneasy relationships with the market dynamics of the publishing industry and public perception, resulting in a mode of canonisation which is inevitably political in its consequences and which produces broader implications for the formation of the geopolitical topographies through which Africa and the world emerge.

It is important at the outset to move through a few cautions and caveats which guide what follows. First and foremost, the idea that African literature is only produced by the major publishing houses of the global North, and that it is primarily produced and disseminated for Euro-American consumption, is by no means an immutable fact. Numerous publishers, writers' collectives, and literary activist organisations continue to proliferate on the African continent, defying the normative vision of a continent under a protracted book famine, with a dearth of reading publics. While Section 3 will contend with some of this material in more depth, it is important to recognise from the outset that the expectation that African literature is, as a matter of course, a product of the

---

[3] James English, *The Economy of Prestige: Prizes, Awards, and the Circulation of Cultural Value* (Cambridge: Harvard University Press, 2005), p. 10.

American, first and foremost, and then European publishing industries is itself a product of a set of intertwined ideological, discursive, and material interests. Indeed, so, too, is the notion that the paradigmatic reader of African literature is its American or British (perhaps sometimes French) consumer; official statistics on readerships on the African continent are difficult to find, given the ways in which continental economies of reading often function through informal channels; yet, my own field work and that of other scholars committed to working coproductively with continental partners shows that rich, vital, and engaged reading cultures exist across its geographies.

For the sake of simplicity, and to minimise the number of scare quotes used in this Element, I therefore use the term 'African literature' to refer to that body of work consecrated and canonised by the global literary market. My use of 'African literary production', by contrast, is intended to capture the larger fullness and diversity of literary activity emanating from the continent and its diasporas. Even a simple discussion of Africa, the physical space, seems doomed to fall into similar forms of confusion from the outset. Africa, the continent, encompasses fifty-five sovereign states and is the second largest continent after Asia; across its totality, it features unparalleled environmental, geographical, linguistic, and cultural diversity. Yet, in its quotidian usage, Africa is often used as an all-encompassing shorthand for sub-Saharan Africa, perpetuating a racialised distinction between the Maghreb and the rest of the continent. Two decades into the twenty-first century, there remains a perception in popular discussions that the continent is little more than an undifferentiated mass, where the Sahel could just as easily be swapped in for the tropical forests of the Equatorial region, or the mountains of the Western Cape for the savannahs of the Great Rift Valley.

In this Element, I mostly discuss English language texts, though each section also contains some discussion of other linguistic contexts. This is largely because, in its current form, the canonical idea of African literature, at least as exists in the academy and the global North, is itself predominantly Anglophone. Sections 1 and 2 of this study focus almost exclusively on the novel form. Again, this is largely due to the ascendency of the novel as the de facto form associated with African literature today. Despite the historical and critical importance of poetry, drama, and short-form fiction on the continent (the latter being of an increasing relevance since the inception in 2000 of the Caine Prize for African Writing, a prize which exclusively considers short stories written or translated into English), the novel has overwhelmingly ascended to become *the* form in which African literature appears. Often ascribed to the success of Achebe's *Things Fall Apart* – a phenomenon which I will discuss in Section 1 – the rise of the novel has served to nearly eclipse other forms. Even the Caine Prize, ostensibly for short stories, is often awarded to a short story conceived of as a chapter of a novel. In Section 3 of this study, I consider in more detail the formal experimentations and shifts which characterise literary production on the continent.

This study is structured in three short sections. The first of these, 'Publishing Africa on a Global Scale', considers the early processes of consecration and canonisation through which African literature emerged into the global literary marketplace. Organised around the two case studies of *Things Fall Apart* and the African Writers Series, it traces the contours of visibility and representation which have consequently shaped perceptions of African writing. The section considers the larger landscape within which these ostensibly foundational moments of African literature occurred and offers alternative stories or narratives through which we might wish to imagine its instantiation. Section 2, 'Contemporary Canons', jumps from the founding moments of African literature to the present day. The 1970s and 1980s marked a period of decline in the African book trade, based on a variety of factors including a global downturn in the production of books, the Nigerian oil crisis, an increase in the price of paper and the withdrawal of state sponsorship for publishing bureaux. Situating the so-called African literary renaissance of the contemporary period against the larger landscape of the neoliberal turn, this section contends with the long-term legacies of what has come to be known as the African book famine in the present day. Here, I draw on close readings of texts by Teju Cole and Chimananda Ngozi Adichie to think about the thematics and aesthetics which drive the consecration of texts as representative of African literature more broadly, and examine the role of the writer-celebrity-spokesperson. In the third and final section of this study, 'Alternative Landscapes', I begin with a consideration of the place of African literature within world literatures more broadly, and then devote the bulk of the section to an exploration of the larger dynamism of African literary production based on the continent. My argument here is that while the range of this work is often rendered illegible and invisible in the institutions and publics of the global North, its excavation in critical and popular study is essential to determining a more robust concept of the literary, as a whole, and the mechanisms of literary activity, production, dissemination, and consecration in Africa and its diasporas.

1 Publishing Africa on a Global Scale

In many accounts, the institution of African literature is intertwined with two particular historical moments: the publication, in 1958, of Chinua Achebe's *Things Fall Apart* and the founding, in 1962, of the Heinemann African Writers Series, of which Achebe's novel served as first title. Both of these events have undeniable significance for the ways in which the canon of African literature has subsequently been formed, particularly with respect to the patterns and politics of visibility which have mediated its constitution over time; yet, as is inevitably the case with origin stories,[4]

---

[4] Robert Fraser, *Book History Through Postcolonial Eyes: Rewriting the Script* (Abingdon: Routledge, 2008), p. 88.

both function less as absolute historical starting points and more as potential sites through which the ideological processes of canon formation and literary valuation might be explored. In Section 1, I focus on these two moments for precisely these reasons, tracing the contours of the normative story of African literature and then offering alternative landscapes through which to consider its demarcations. Across these arguments, my aim is to foreground the dynamics of visibility which have accompanied the dominant narrative of African literature's creation and constitution, and which continue to bear upon the ways in which it is positioned in the global literary field.

In 1957 Chinua Achebe, then a young broadcaster on a training course in London, approached Gilbert Phelps with a manuscript detailing a multigenerational saga of Igbo life from the first moments of contact with European colonisers to the era of anticolonial independence struggles. Heavily revised and overhauled, this manuscript would transform into the author's first three novels, *Things Fall Apart* (1958), *No Longer at Ease* (1960), and *Arrow of God* (1964). With two novels tracing the life and fall of Okonkwo, a strongman famed across the nine villages of Umuofia, located in the southeast of present-day Nigeria, and the subsequent corruption of his grandson, Obi Okonkwo, a 'been-to' caught between conflicting ideologies during the period immediately around self-rule and independence, and the third telling the story of Ezeulu, the embattled spiritual leader of his tribe in the intervening years of high colonisation, the trilogy has collectively been positioned as the foundation upon which African literature has been built, with its first instalment credited variously with its establishment as a category operating within the global literary field. As James Currey, reflecting on its publication in the African Writers Series, notes, 'If people have read one novel from Africa it is most likely that it will have been *Things Fall Apart*. Sales in English may well have passed 10 million. There have been translations into almost fifty other languages. It now appears in Penguin Modern Classics'.[5] Unparalleled in its visibility as a representative of African literature, writ large, the novel is notable for several features: its integration of Igbo language and terminology and cultural and religious customs, including descriptions of ritual practice, religious rites, family ceremonies, folktales, and collective governance; its depiction of a humanised African personality, something which might be read as a rebuff to the European vision of the continent in which, as Achebe himself once lamented, Africa functions as mere 'setting and backdrop which eliminates the African as human factor';[6] its use of proverbs and idioms derived from – and sometimes reproduced in – the Igbo language; its adaptation of modernist forms and conventions, including, of course, its very title, a quotation from Yeats's poem 'The Second Coming', which serves as an epigraph to the novel; and more. Despite the novel's relatively modest length, moreover, set over three parts following Okonkwo from Umuofia to his exile in Mbanta and eventual return, the text features a densely populated world far removed from the alien land devoid of humanity once described in the works of Conrad and his contemporaries.

It is not my intention here to dwell upon the relative worth of Achebe's text as a literary work; there exists a broad body of scholarship which does precisely this.[7] Rather, my interest in this discussion is to consider the ways in

[5] James Currey, *Africa Writes Back: The African Writers Series and the Launch of African Literature* (Athens: Ohio University Press, 2008), p. 28.

[6] Chinua Achebe, *Hopes and Impediments: Selected Essays* (New York: Anchor, 1988), p. 12.

[7] See, for instance, Simon Gikandi, 'Chinua Achebe and the Invention of African Culture', *Research in African Literatures*, 32.3 (2001): 3–8; Stephanie Newell, *West African Literature: Ways of Reading* (Oxford: Oxford University Press, 2006); James Olney, 'The African Novel in Transition: Chinua Achebe', *South Atlantic Quarterly*, 70 (1971): 299–316; Dan Izevbaye, 'Chinua Achebe and the African Novel',

which the text has been positioned – seemingly intractably – as the founding text of African literature and the implications which so arise for how we think about African literature as a category. In many ways, the publication of *Things Fall Apart* has become something of a myth in itself. In an essay which appears in the author's last published volume, Achebe describes at length the process which led to his drafting of the novel:

> I worked on my writing mostly at night. I was seized by the story and I found myself totally ensconced in it. It was almost like living in a parallel realm, a dual existence not in any negative sense but in the way a hand has two surfaces, united in purpose but very different in tone, appearance, character, and structure.[8]

In these comments, Achebe invokes the aura now so often attributed to *Things Fall Apart*, describing the process of writing the novel as an experience of the sublime, another existence running in parallel with his daily life as a young broadcaster at the Nigerian Broadcasting Company. Recounting how he nearly lost the manuscript after sending it to be typed out by an unscrupulous London agency eager to take advantage of the young Nigerian, only rescued from the dustbin of history by the interventions of one of Achebe's colleagues, a former BBC Talks producer, Achebe's recollections continue to trace the unlikely trajectory through which the novel would eventually travel. In many ways, *Things Fall Apart*'s origin story is remarkable: a young Nigerian broadcaster,

in *The Cambridge Companion to the African Novel*, ed. by F. Abiola Irele (Cambridge: Cambridge University Press, 2009), pp. 31–50.

[8] Chinua Achebe, *There Was A Country: A Personal History of Biafra* (London: Allen Lane, 2012), p. 35.

never having previously left his country and sent on a training course to London, shows a manuscript to an acquaintance; awed by what he has seen, said acquaintance passes the manuscript on, becoming its advocate and supporter; relentlessly rejected and diminished for its provenance, the manuscript finally finds a home, consecrated through the recommendation of a reliable area studies expert. Here, then, is a story of happenstance and providence, mediated by a range of benevolent gatekeepers whose ultimate support would result in the publication of *Things Fall Apart*, changing the course of literary history as we know it. This is in itself something at which to marvel, and the continual retelling of this story is indicative of the mythic status to which the novel has ascended and, with it, the mythic status of African literature itself.

The reception of *Things Fall Apart* can be characterised by a positioning of the novel as an authentic document of Igbo culture and society in the nineteenth century, a riposte to the distorted vision of the continent rendered in British depictions.[9] Early reviews of the novel laud the ways in which it constitutes 'a fascinating picture of tribal life among [the author's] own people at the end of the nineteenth century',[10] 'tak[ing] its place with that small company of sensitive books that describe primitive society from the inside',[11] 'intimately present[ing] this medley of mores of the Ibo tribe',[12] all while rendered in a 'clear and meaty style free of [. . .] dandyism'.[13] Across geographies reviews focus

---

[9] See Dorothy Hammond and Alta Jablow, *The Africa that Never Was: Four Centuries of British Writing about Africa* (Prospect Heights, NY: Waveland Press, 1992).

[10] Philip Stanley Rawson, 'The Centre Cannot Hold', *Times Literary Supplement*, 20 June 1958, p. 341.

[11] Selden Rodman, 'The White Man's Faith', *New York Times Book Review*, 22 February 1959, p. 28.

[12] Hassoldt Davis, 'Jungle Strongman', *Saturday Review*, 31 January 1959, p. 18.

[13] Review in *The Listener*, quoted in David Borman, 'Playful Ethnography: Chinua Achebe's *Things Fall Apart* and Nigerian Education', *ARIEL: A Review of*

almost uniformly on the authenticity and educational value of Achebe's portrayal of Umuofian life, citing its 'simple story of an African village hero against a rich canvas of African village and tribal life';[14] praising it for its 'glimpses of old African village customs and practices, down to details of domestic life';[15] casting approval on the universalism and accuracy of Achebe's depiction of the African world;[16] and arguing that 'secondary children will get more of old Nigeria from this than from ten text-books'.[17]

The tendency to read literary texts as providing anthropological and sociological data in an untroubled manner is not unique to African literature. Yet, there is a certain intensity to this process when applied to the African context, fabricating larger links between the practice of reading and the longer discursive histories around which Africa has come to be in a global imaginary. As Mbembe notes,

> European discourse, both scholarly and popular, had a way of
> thinking, of classifying and imagining distant worlds, that was

International English Literature, 46.3 (2015), 91–112. For more on the reception of *Things Fall Apart*, see Borman; Carey Snyder, 'The Possibilities and Pitfalls of Ethnographic Readings: Narrative Complexity in *Things Fall Apart*', *College Literature*, 35.2 (2008), 154–75; Raoul Granqvist, 'The Early Swedish Reviews of Chinua Achebe's *Things Fall Apart* and *A Man of the People*', *Research in African Literatures*, 15.3 (1984), 394–404.

[14] Ian Hope, 'Life and Letters: *Things Fall Apart*', Radio Singapura, 12 September 1966. Transcript accessed at the University of Reading Special Collections, Heinemann Educational Books, African Writers Series.

[15] Ibid.

[16] 'Paperback of the Week', 17 July 1962. Press clipping accessed at the University of Reading Special Collections, Heinemann Educational Books, African Writers Series.

[17] Windsor Grammar School, 'Prelude'. Press clipping accessed at the University of Reading Special Collections, Heinemann Educational Books, African Writers Series.

often based on modes of fantasizing. By presenting facts, often invented, as real, certain, and exact, it evaded what it claimed to capture and maintained a relationship to other worlds that was fundamentally imaginary, even as it sought to develop forms of knowledge aimed at representing them objectively.[18]

This discursive phenomenon, based on the dual play of determined ignorance and total authority, directly connects the linguistic, narrative, and ideological positioning of the continent through rhetoric to the larger modes of violence and exploitation produced through the slave trade, colonialism, and neoliberalisation. The tendency to view African literature, moreover, as authenticating disinterested, but factually true, knowledge operates within this same conceptual matrix, with the same potential to lead to mastery, domination, and a continuation, ironically, of the same modes of ignorant authority as have historically determined the continent's place in the world. While I do not wish, in Brouillette's terms, to 'subscrib[e] to a logic that separates the authentic from the inauthentic, the insider from the outsider, in an endless cycle of hierarchical distinction and counter-distinction',[19] my argument in this section is that the historical concordances which emerge between the positioning of African literature and the longer history of discourse around the African continent raise important questions around the dynamics of visibility through which the literary field functions, and particularly the tensions and negotiations which constitute the network of relations upon which it relies.

---

[18] Achille Mbembe, *A Critique of Black Reason*, translated by Laurent Dubois (Durham: Duke University Press, 2017), p. 12.

[19] Sarah Brouillette, *Postcolonial Writers in the Global Literary Marketplace* (Basingstoke: Palgrave Macmillan, 2005), p. 19.

Despite the tendency to read *Things Fall Apart* in historical-realist terms which privilege the reception of the text as a site of authentic, insider information, its status as a work of fiction remains evident in its deeper interpretation. Scholars ranging from Stephanie Newell to Rhonda Cobham Sanders have noted the ways in which Achebe alternately foregrounds the ultimate untranslatability of the novel, its imaginative reconstruction of historical and cultural facts, and its deliberate play with the referentiality of meaning.[20] Within the novel, for instance, remain a series of episodes and asides which the narrative refuses to decipher to their full transparent comprehensibility: from its invocation of the kola nut ritual in its opening pages, complete with never-again mentioned references to the drawing of lines and painting of the big toe in chalk by a visitor to Okonkwo's father;[21] to references to the ceremonial *egwugwu* masked dancers, the figure of the *ogbanje* and their cursed *iyi-uwa* (80–1); depictions of marriage ceremonies and the *umuada* and *umunna* (societies of women and men, respectively, with important roles in the administration of law, order, and justice in the clan), Achebe's novel is rife with instances which frustrate the epistemophillic function supposed to drive the anthropological impulse in reading the text.[22] Equally, the narrative's own textual form is peppered with references to other modes of discursive contact, most notably in the repeated resonance of nonverbal modes of communication in the form of the *ogene*, the *ekwe*, and the drum. At one point described as 'the pulsation of

---

[20] Rhonda Cobham Sanders, 'Problems of Gender and History in the Teaching of *Things Fall Apart*', in *Chinua Achebe's Things Fall Apart: A Casebook*, ed. by Isidore Okpewho (New York: Oxford University Press, 2003), pp. 165–80; Newell, pp. 85–100.

[21] Chinua Achebe, *Things Fall Apart* (New York: Anchor, 1994 [1958]), p. 6. All subsequent references to this edition cited in text.

[22] See, for example, Graham Huggan, *The Postcolonial Exotic: Marketing the Margins* (London: Routledge, 2001).

[the village's] heart', which 'throbbed in the air, in the sunshine, and even in trees, and filled the village with excitement' (44), the repeated play of these elements indicates the existence of a model of communication utterly known to the villagers and yet completely untranslatable within the frame of the narrative itself. Tellingly, in the first invocation of the *ogene*, the novel follows the instrument's throbbing beat with the information, never directly rendered, that the town crier gave his message, itself relegated to a textual gloss which indicates the very partiality and incompletion of the act of translation itself and, at the same time, the incommensurability and intangibility of true comprehension.

The novel, as Newell has aptly demonstrated, is rife with such moments which foreground that which is unresolvable and unrecoverable.[23] Early in the text, for instance, we learn that the pejorative *agbala*, literally 'another name for a woman' bears another meaning and 'could also mean a man who has taken no title' (13). Yet, mere pages later we are introduced to one of the central figures in the organisation of village life, Agbala, the Oracle of the Hills and Caves (16), the priestess who stands at once as the fiercest, most potent, and most feared of the village's spiritual leaders on the one hand, and as an ordinary widow with two children on the other (49). In a pivotal scene, the narrative describes the fevered rush with which Ekwefi, Okonkwo's beloved second wife, follows the priestess, Chielo, through the lands surrounding the village at night, desperate to know the fate of her daughter, the *ogbanje* child Ezinma. Travelling for untold hours and miles, Ekwefi's focalised perspective makes plain the irreducibility of Chielo's duality: 'How a woman could carry a child of that size so easily and for so long was a miracle. But Ekwefi was not thinking about that. Chielo was not a woman that night' (107). Indeed, in their respective readings both Newell and Brown cite the untranslability of *Things Fall Apart* as

[23] Newell, p. 96.

a novel saturated with an excess in the shape of Igbo cultural practices, registered through a mode of language which refuses to collapse alternative possibilities and meanings. Instead, the novel plays with 'a distance placed between a totalising narrative and individual agency that is allowed to be infinite and unknowable' and an ethnographic, anthropological practice 'in which the untranslatable, or unrecoverable, elements of a culture are kept as such, without being filtered through "global" explanatory frameworks'.[24] Igbo culture itself is presented in heterogeneous terms, highlighted in the villagers' bemusement at the ritual practices of their neighbours, with their 'upside-down' customs (73); the humour produced by the literal impossibility of total mutual comprehension across a people and a land of multiple dialects (144); and the singularity of the individual characters who populate its world. Despite incontrovertible textual evidence against the anthropological reading, that the novel has so consistently been positioned as an untroubled social document indicates the ways in which its position functions precisely through the processes described by Mbembe, as more broadly characteristic of the African continent's positioning in global imaginary. The rhetoric accompanying it and the power of normative reading practices serve to reinforce its strength.

Discussions of African literature often cite Achebe's own efforts to position the social value of his work as a writer. In 'The Novelist as Teacher', first published in *The New Statesman* in 1965 and subsequently reprinted in multiple collections of the author's essays and criticism, Achebe outlines his vision of the African writer's social commitment as one of 're-education' and 'regeneration'.[25] In an oft-cited passage, he describes his own ambition 'to teach [his] readers that their past – with all its imperfections – was

---

[24] Nicholas Brown, *Utopian Generations: The Political Horizon of Twentieth-Century Literature* (Princeton: Princeton University Press, 2005), p. 117; Newell, p. 96.

[25] Achebe, *Hopes and Impediments*, p. 45.

not one long night of savagery from which the first Europeans acting on God's behalf delivered them'.[26] Achebe's comments fall within the specific context of *Things Fall Apart*'s dissemination and reception, a context which challenges many of the precepts through which we view the global literary market and the positioning of African literature therein. As he explains in that same essay, *Things Fall Apart*, for all of its critical acclaim in Britain and America, remained best-selling in Nigeria itself; in the year before the publication of that essay, Achebe cites the following figures: 'the pattern of sales of *Things Fall Apart* in cheap paperback edition was as follows: about 800 copies in Britain; 20,000 in Nigeria; and about 2,500 in all other places. The same pattern was true also of *No Longer at Ease*'.[27] Elsewhere in that same essay, Achebe reproduces the full text of a letter from a young admirer, a student who, in his appreciative note, compliments the author and his works for 'serv[ing] as advice to us young'.[28] For Achebe, the meaning is clear, and by no means isolated. Indeed, similar sentiments are reported by Newell, whose 1998 interviews with young Ghanaian readers of the novel repeatedly cite [Achebe's] ability to "educate" them about "traditional ways of life" as a key element of his art.[29] Given that *Things Fall Apart* was, from 1966, a set text for the O Level English examination in West Africa,[30] it is perhaps unsurprising that the novel should be so evaluated; still more importantly, however, and as Newell notes, 'different aesthetic values [...] prevail in different localities, conditioning readers' expectations and causing many, as in Ghana [and Nigeria], to *expect* to extract

---

[26] Achebe, *Hopes and Impediments*, p. 45. [27] Achebe, *Hopes and Impediments*, p. 41.

[28] Achebe, *Hopes and Impediments*, pp. 41–2. [29] Newell, p. 96.

[30] *Things Fall Apart* was also a prescribed book by the Joint Matriculation Board in apartheid South Africa from 1975.

both truths and lessons from a text'.[31] In a context where educational value is expected to come from the text, that is, it is not in the least surprising that so many of the young readers cited in the 1960s by Achebe and in the 1990s by Newell should seek out some form of re-education through their encounter with *Things Fall Apart*; at the same time, these expectations cannot be said to be entirely analogous with those of metropolitan readers in their ultimate valuation and implications, suggesting the simultaneous existence of a critical reading account oriented elsewhere.

In 1962, *Things Fall Apart* was republished as the first offering in the nascent African Writers Series, published by Heinemann Educational Books, and Achebe appointed its first Editorial Adviser, responsible for sourcing and evaluating potential manuscripts and promising writers. Achebe's appointment to this role, much like the publication of his first novel, has become something of a mythic moment in the history of African literature. James Currey, who spearheaded the series from 1967 to 1984, writes:

> In that very year of the start of the Series, 1962, there was a conference on African writing at Makerere University College in Uganda in July. Chinua Achebe heard a knock at the door of his guest house in the evening and found a student standing there who offered him the manuscripts of two novels. The name of the Kenyan student was Ngũgĩ [wa Thiong'o].[32]

Again, as in the story of *Things Fall Apart*'s original publication, happenstance and providence meet a willing gatekeeper, and so emerges a pivotal moment in the development of African literature as we know it today, impossible to

[31] Newell, p. 97. [32] Currey, p. 3

imagine were it not for Achebe's patronage and support. Following that meeting, Achebe strongly supported the publication of Ngũgĩ's *Weep Not, Child*, number seven in the African Writers Series, leading to the older author's appointment as Editorial Adviser for the series and, following his retirement from this role, the title of Founding Editor.

In a 1998 lecture at Harvard, Achebe likens the 'launching of the Heinemann's African Writers Series' to an 'umpire's signal for which African writers had been waiting on the starting line'.[33] In many contemporary accounts, these statements have come to function as shorthand to describe the origins of the African literary canon, saturated with the language of historical compression and a retrospectively anticipatory temporality. Reading these comments, one might be forgiven for assuming that the years prior to the institution of the African Writers Series were little more than a vacuum, an 'expectant, Achebe-shaped pause' in which little activity of any merit occurred.[34] The story of African literature most visible in the global North, that is, is one in which the African Writers Series is positioned as a necessary measure intended to fill a market gap, providing an outlet for aspiring writers from the continent and introducing their work to the global stage upon which capital is supposed to be accrued. This is a story founded on a discursive matrix which speaks to the dual imperative of obligation and necessity which was so frequently deployed in the rhetoric of the civilising mission, rife with commentary that the series 'wanted to persuade that industry take writing by Africans seriously';[35] that 'the African Writers Series set out to give Africans the freedom to write back';[36] that the Series, contra the tendency towards 'Afropessimism', enabled the African writers to 'reach [. . .] out across the world' and more,[37] solidifying the sense that the Series was a necessary precondition

---

[33] Chinua Achebe, *Home and Exile* (New York: Oxford University Press, 2000), p. 51.
[34] Newell, p. 98. [35] Currey, p. 9. [36] Currey, p. 21. [37] Currey, p. 24.

for the valuation of African literature in a global literary field still oriented around a centre/periphery axis. And yet, as Achebe's own trajectory – and that of the Series more broadly – indicates, this is far from a simple historical truth, simply one story among many, endowed perhaps with a particular mode of visibility but far from the only possible tale to tell.

In *An Ecology of World Literature*, Alexander Beecroft argues that it is 'in the world of audiences or readers that the notion of a literature really emerges'. Under this reading, literatures 'are techniques or practices of reading texts, and specifically of linking texts together, through a series of relationships that usually begins with language and/or the polity, but which also include questions of genre and influence, among other criteria' and which 'take on meaningful form only when there are texts excluded from them'.[38] The insights which Beecroft's observations produce are important for enabling a vision of canon formation as a dialectical process of connection and exclusion through which a given version of a literature – limited, partial, strategic, or contingent as it may be – becomes naturalised in its appearance as an essential and timeless whole. Through the tension produced between, on the one hand, the modes of citation which enable connections and links across a body of work to transpire and, on the other, the erasures and exclusions which consecrate that body of work as totalised whole, this reading of canon formation opens up a space in which the practices of visibility might become evident. Here, I turn to a recent keynote address delivered by Moradewun Adejunmobi, titled 'African Writing and the Forms of Publicness'.[39] In this lecture, Adejunmobi draws an important distinction between the notions of publicness and visibility. Crucially for

[38] Alexander Beecroft, *An Ecology of World Literature: From Antiquity to the Present Day* (London: Verso, 2014), p. 17.

[39] Moradewun Adejunmobi, 'African Writing and the Forms of Publicness', keynote lecture at the Small Magazines, Literary Networks and Self-Fashioning in Africa and its Diasporas conference, 19 January 2018, Bristol, United Kingdom.

my purposes here is the iterative nature through which that which is public becomes – and remains – visible, requiring a continual recurrence of citation, reference, and reproduction much in the same way as the accrual of capital in the literary field does. To understand this process, one might wish to consider an example such as that of Yambo Ouologuem's *Le devoir de violence* (published in 1968 by Éditions de Seuil and translated to English as *Bound to Violence* in 1971). The recipient of the 1968 Prix Renaudot, one of France's most prestigious literary prizes, the novel was originally lauded for its sweeping historical account of present-day Mali from the thirteenth century to the period immediately preceding independence, its author acclaimed as an intellectual giant on par with Léopold Sédar Senghor. The novel itself produces an invective exploration of the dynamics of power, violence, and eroticism which span across eras, developing an unflinching critique of the politics of assimilation in the colonial era and the recurrent 'négraille' ingrained within black populations. Despite its critical success, the novel fell prey to controversy when 'seeming translations and adaptations of excerpts from novels by Graham Greene, André Schwarz-Bart, and Guy de Maupassant, as well as other works were soon discerned within the text',[40] which opened the author to charges of plagiarism.[41] The novel was subsequently banned in France, where it remains out of print – and literally rendered invisible – today.

Central to Adejenmobi's arguments is the observation that when a work attracts citation as part of critical discourse, its visibility increases.

[40] Kyle Wanberg, 'Ghostwriting History: Subverting the Reception of *Le regard du roi* and *Le devoir de violence*', *Comparative Literature Studies*, 50.4 (2013), 598–617 (p. 610).

[41] See Eric Sellin, 'Ouologuem's Blueprint for *Le devoir de violence*', *Research in African Literatures*, 2.2 (1971), 117–20; Robert McDonald, 'Bound to Violence: A Case of Plagiarism', *Transition*, 41 (1972), 64–8.

At the same time, alternative streams of citationality – and alternative literary public spheres – continue to function in spaces, landscapes, and forms which might not be endowed with the same modes of visibility as those associated with the global literary field. Returning to *Le devoir*, for instance, one might consider the ways in which the novel has remained a central text in academic discourse around Francophone African writing, particularly within the Anglophone sphere where its continued visibility might be attributed in part to its publication in translation as part of the African Writers Series. If the contours of a literature, following Beecroft, are constituted through the practices of connectivity and exclusion driven by readerships, it moreover remains true that other, less visible, options remain open and engaged. Recalling Bourdieu's insight that value and capital, however relational, remain finite resources subject to competition, the insights derived from Beecroft's and Adejunmobi's arguments may allow us to perceive the ways in which the literary field functions not as a single entity, but as multiple, overlapping, sometimes conflictual frames differently endowed with visibility and legibility across spatiotemporal mooring points. The iterative nature of both canon formation and the practices of visibility make it evident that these contours shift over time and place, evolving and reforming in different measure.

In the case of the African Writers Series, several other positionings remain possible, their perceptibility dependent on the publics to which any given interpreter has access and, by extension, the citational-critical frameworks made available. Despite the tendency to position the series as the beginning of African literature, the 'umpire's signal', in Achebe's words, it is possible to view the series in relation to a host of other institutions and networks operational both before and after its inception. James Currey, for instance, prior to his role with the Series, served with Randolph Vigne as editor of *The New African*, a radical literary magazine based initially in Cape

Town and then London,[42] which from 1962 published writing by individuals differently endowed with visibility across discrepant public spheres. With names including Bessie Head, Lewis Nkosi, Ngũgĩ, Dennis Brutus, André Brink, Nadine Gordimer, and Alan Paton, the magazine's published authors include many who would go on to work with the African Writers Series. Placing the Series in dialogue with this archive, then, better enables us to position it as one element in a far broader, if uneven and asymmetrically loaded, literary field comprised of missionary and educational presses;[43] popular fiction; ephemeral and occasional literature such as that associated with Onitsha and Ghana market pamphlet culture;[44] small magazines such as the aforementioned *The New African*, as well as foundational radical periodicals like *Black Orpheus* and *Transition*; university and school literary societies;[45] Afrophone and other Europhone literary histories;[46] and even those novels, such as Amos Tutuola's *The Palm-Wine Drinkard* (published by

---

[42] *The New African* was forced to move premises following extended harassment from the apartheid government. Full details of this historical account are available in James Currey and Randolph Vigne, *The New African: A History* (London: Merlin Press, 2014).

[43] See Fraser; Mũkoma wa Ngũgĩ, *The Rise of the African Novel: Politics of Language, Identity and Ownership* (Ann Arbor: University of Michigan Press, 2018).

[44] See Newell; Karin Barber (ed.), *Readings in African Popular Culture* (London: The International African Institute, 1997); Derek R. Peterson, Emma Hunter, and Stephanie Newell (eds), *African Print Cultures: Newspapers and Their Publics in the Twentieth Century* (Ann Arbor: University of Michigan Press, 2016).

[45] See Terri Ochiagha, *Achebe and Friends at Umuahia: The Making of a Literary Elite* (Oxford: James Currey, 2015).

[46] See Ruth Bush, *Publishing Africa in French* (Liverpool: University of Liverpool Press, 2016); Claire Ducournau, *La fabrique des classiques africaines* (Paris: CNRS Éditions, 2017).

Faber and Faber in 1952), which came before. If we imagine that African literature began with the 1962 Makerere conference and the institution of the African Writers Series, moreover, it is equally important to recall the wider network of institutional relationships which have enabled their visibility as such.[47] One significant example is the 1963 Fourah Bay conference of teachers of English from the Anglophone sphere, at which the value of African literature in the educational curriculum was debated. It was this conference which led to the formation of a powerful lobbying body able to put books by African writers – often, because of its focus on low-cost educational editions, those published in the Series – on English literature syllabi across the continent, enabling a constant and recurring process of citation and reading which would drive its formation as a literature on par with canonical works by Shakespeare and Dickens.[48] In the Francophone sphere, by contrast, a similar conference held in Dakar came to the opposite conclusion, consigning Francophone African literature to the anthropology department, only available as 'literature' through its translation to English. The different conclusions drawn at these two conferences continue to shape the visibility of African literature today, contributing to the continued dominance of Anglophone writing in education, scholarship, and the popular imagination in much the same manner as the centrality of Paris in the publishing of

---

[47] For instance, *The New African*, *Transition*, *Black Orpheus*, and the Makerere Conference were all variously funded by the Congress for Cultural Freedom, whose parent organisation, the Farfield Foundation, operated as a front for the CIA with an interest in promoting anticommunist cultural ideologies. Available interview material with journal editors and organisers suggests that, despite this, the Foundation put no pressure on publishers to censor material.

[48] James Currey, 'Ngũgĩ, Leeds and the Establishment of African Literature', *Leeds African Studies Bulletin*, 74 (2012), 48–62 (pp. 48–9).

Francophone African literature versus the relatively more dispersed structures available to Anglophone authors.[49]

There is too often today a tendency to view processes of canonisation and literary historiography, which are at their heart contingent, as immutable historical truths. To a certain degree, this reflects the potency of fossilised disciplinary and institutional structures which continue to mediate the kinds of scholarship – and storytelling – that is possible. It should be fairly clear by now, however, that, like all origin stories, the story of *Things Fall Apart*, the African Writers Series, and the emergence of African literature might be said to occlude as much as it illuminates. More than simply explicating some disinterested notion of the emergence and development of African literature, prima facie, what emerges in this story gestures more towards a series of observations about the social, political, and ideological precepts which undergird the dialectics of connection and exclusion and the citational processes of visibility. These all continue to shape the contours of the story of African literature; a story which, moreover, is inextricably linked to larger discourses around 'Africa' in the global imagination, from the colonial era to the present day. Returning to *Things Fall Apart*, then, one might wonder what would happen to our conception of African literature if, rather than view the text as its founding gambit, the novel were seen as simultaneously existing against a range of discrepant, sometimes overlapping and sometimes conflictual literary genealogies and entanglements potentially less visible in the global North but perceptible elsewhere. *Things Fall Apart* might productively be seen as arising from a form of late modernist writing, situated within a larger context of global black modernisms including the writers of the Harlem Renaissance, Sam Selvon's *The Lonely*

---

[49] The African Writers Series, for instance, functioned through a triangulated editorial process with offices in Ibadan, Nairobi, and London. This is in direct contrast to the Francophone publishing sector, where editorial control remained centred on Paris.

Londoners, and fellow African and African diaspora writers such as Wole Soyinka, Christopher Okigbo (a close friend of Achebe's until the time of his death in the Nigerian-Biafran War and cofounder with the author of Citadel Press) and Achebe's fellows in the Mbari Club. Equally, the novel might be seen, following Nicholas Brown's reading, as 'reinvent[ing] "the classic form of the historical novel" in the precise Lukácsian sense', placed in a genre and genealogy with Sir Walter Scott's *Waverly*, James Fenimore Cooper's *The Leather Stocking Saga*, or Gogol's *Taras Bulba*.[50] Through its references to Tennyson, Yeats, and others, moreover, Achebe's novel not only enters into a dialogue with canonical English literature, but it also forces a revisioning of the ideological complexes at the heart of that body of work, 'so dense with cross-references to European canonical texts and imperial writings that Achebe appears to be deliberately avoiding an assertion of cultural "authenticity" in order to debate the more complicated issue of Africa's inscription into colonial discourse'.[51]

Like the African Writers Series which it founded, *Things Fall Apart* might also be read within a longer genealogy of print culture which encompassed religious pamphlets, popular fiction, self-help texts and, of course, small magazines. Notably for any discussion of the canonisation of African literature, popular and pamphlet literature did not function entirely as a world apart, with major contributors to the genre including Achebe's own countryman, Cyprian Ekwensi, who went on in 1954 to publish *People of the City*, a novel based on a series of short stories and vignettes recorded by the author for the BBC's African Voices programme. Originally published in London by Andrew Dakers, *People of the City* would eventually be revised and rereleased as the fifth title in the African Writers Series, complicating the narrative so-often told which reduces these pre-Achebian moments to little more than a blip. Achebe

---

[50] Brown, p. 104. [51] Newell, p. 90.

himself might be positioned within this longer print history, notably through his involvement with literary culture in his days as a student at Government College Umuahia.[52] Significantly, many of his fellows from this period, including Christopher Okigbo, would go on to publish in the leading pan-Africanist literary journal *Black Orpheus*. In a context where small magazines and literary journals flourished,[53] *Black Orpheus* remains a significant platform through which literary production was engendered and mediated. Founded in 1957 by German expatriate Ulli Beier, *Black Orpheus* soon became an important node in transnational, translingual, and pan-African literary production, inspired by the Paris-based *Présence Africaine* and conceiving of itself as 'an experimental workshop and gallery for new artists and writers'.[54] The activities around the magazine eventually coalesced into the creation of the Ibadan-based Mbari Club, of which Achebe, along with figures like Okigbo, Wole Soyinka, J. P. Clarke, and others, was a member. Both a physical space located in Ibadan and Oshogbo and crucible for literary activities, the club eventually formed a publishing house based in Ibadan, which saw the release of landmark works of African literature.

Black Orpheus, in particular, was known for publishing work from the Americas and the Francophone world in translation; this, too, points to a longer history of interaction and accordance between the allegedly discrete diasporic, Anglophone, and Francophone spheres. While literary scholarship today often views these latter areas as discrete, the first half of the twentieth century was notable for the ways in which writers from across the continent, irrespective of

---

[52] See Ochiagha.

[53] A brief list of some of the magazines and journals which flourished from the 1950s to 1970s includes *Transition, Darlite, Busara, Joe, Penpoints, Zuka, Okike*, among countless more.

[54] Peter Benson, *Black Orpheus, Transition and Modern Cultural Awakening in Africa* (Berkeley: University of California Press, 1986), p. 1.

linguistic difference, operated within a network of collaboration that continued into the postindependence years, evidenced in the four major pan-African festivals which shaped public culture on the continent held in Dakar (1966), Algiers (1969), Kinshasa (1974), and Lagos (1977), respectively. If we consider the thematic and formal qualities of this work, moreover, a range of productive concordances and discrepancies emerge which attest to the shifting contours of literary production on the continent. Novels such as Laye's *L'enfant noir* and Kane's *L'aventure ambiguë*, for instance, participate in much of the same work of cultural reconstitution as seen in Achebe's oeuvre, enlivening a vision of a rural world steeped in complex traditions, discourses, and social dynamics. At the same time, these texts offer a different possibility for interpreting the modes of cultural negotiation which characterised the colonial era, developing, in Laye, a critical-nostalgic account marked by a retrospective sense of loss and, in Kane, the longue durée of entanglements and displacements which have marked the African continent's being-in-the-world. In both cases, moreover, the picture of assimilation through colonial education offers a distinct means for critiquing the culturalist account of African literature, simultaneously centralising the Parisian metropole as a site of alienation while providing an outlet through which to perceive the dynamism of traditions, norms, and internal heterogeneity of the West African nation-state.[55] Reading these works in

---

[55] In Laye, for instance, the narrative foregrounds the heterogeneity of space ranging across the narrator's home village of Kouroussa, his maternal home of Tindican and his musings, on preparing to depart to the capital to continue his education, that 'le fait que Conakry est la capitale de la Guinée, ne faisait qu'accentuer le caractère d'étrangeté du lieu où je me rendrais' (Camara Laye, *L'enfant noir* [Paris: Librairie Plon, 1953], p. 156); for a substantial discussion on the constitution of spatial multiplicities in Kane, see Madhu Krishnan, 'From Empire to Independence: Colonial Space in the Writing of Tutuola, Ekwensi, Beti, and Kane', *Comparative Literature Studies*, 54.2 (2017), 329–57.

concert with Achebe's, then, allows a more nuanced picture of the agonistic processes and diverse landscapes which have characterised the continent over time to emerge, enabling fuller and more robust readings of the past through specifically aesthetic strategies of representation.

Much of my attention in this section has remained on Achebe, the African Writers Series, and the founding myths of African literature as it currently exists in the global literary field. While there are, I believe, good reasons for so doing, it is equally possible that my own critical account of the institution of African literature might be held to account for doing precisely what it purports to challenge and reinforcing the puissance of these so-called founding moments and singular narrative. In what remains of Section 1, then, I wish to turn my attention to one instance out of what are potentially many that exemplifies the type of work which does not fit so neatly into the most visible story of African literature, Dambudzo Marechera's *The House of Hunger*. A collection centred on the eponymous novella, *The House of Hunger* was originally published in 1978 as the 207th title in the African Writers Series. If Achebe came to be positioned as one of the original 'conspirators' in the establishment of African literature,[56] Marechera's positioning, too, is telling, based not on the premises of accommodation, cooperation, and compromise which that term implies, but on an aggressive – and often bewildering – rejection of its very precepts. In *Africa Writes Back*, Currey recounts the difficulties which his relationship with Marechera – what he characterises as 'the Marechera saga' – entailed,[57] recounting a fraught set of interactions which continued over the years. Tellingly, two very different interpretations of the relationship between author and publisher are juxtaposed; the one, recounted by Marechera's former lover

[56] Currey, p. 24. [57] Curry, p. xix.

and biographer, Flora Veit-Wild, characterised as that of a wayward son and 'surrogate father',[58] and the other as one of torment and antagonism:

> [Veit-Wild] also uses the word 'friendship' about our [Currey's and Marechera's] relationship. I never chose to be with Dambudzo Marechera except for professional reasons. To be near him was to be on red alert. The curtain was always about to go up on some new drama which totally absorbed one's time. I always tried to keep a professional distance so that I could help him put together an income on which to survive. I needed to protect my time to look after my many other authors, several of whom really had become personal friends.[59]

Elsewhere recalling how 'when you were with Dambudzo Marechera your middle-class training was in suspense',[60] Currey's recollections are telling for what they imply around the various positions taken, attributed to, and held by the different actors involved. At once a 'searing talent' and a threat to extant notions of the place of the African writer (as Currey recounts, one report from Kenya notes that 'the writer does not have a high opinion of the black man. He is pompous and a bore, trying to fight liberation from Western capitals while all the time wishing that he was white'),[61] giving 'journalists enough copy to make their readers feel guilty about the treatment of Africans under the [Ian] Smith regime [in Rhodesia]' and plaguing those 'burdened with liberal consciences',[62] Marechera emerges from these pages as a figure both ungovernable and uninterested in adopting the vaunted Achebean role of the writer as teacher and sage. Internal documents and correspondence regarding Marechera from

[58] Currey, p. 280. [59] Currey, p. 280. [60] Currey, p. 290. [61] Currey, p. 281.
[62] Currey, p. 290; p. 288.

the Heinemann archives emphasise this point: marked by regular episodes of trouble with the law, fallings out with supporters, friends, and landlords and a refusal to conform to any sense of social norms, the Marechera which emerges in these documents is best summed up in the warning sent by Currey to the author's American publishers that 'THIS MAN IS DANGEROUS [. . .] to himself'.[63]

There is little point in speculating about the full range of issues which plagued Marechera's personal and professional life in these years. What interests me instead is the extent to which Marechera, as a figure, defies the easy ordering and conviviality which characterises so much of the dominant story of African literature. 'The House of Hunger' is itself a text which is difficult to position within an easy genealogy proceeding in a straight line from Achebe. The titular story is a tale invested not with a nostalgic or objective assessment of past times or a desire to teach and empower, told instead from a feverish first-person perspective inundated with the rage inhered by colonialist violence and its aftermaths. Moving from township to shanty to bar, it acts as a text which refuses all enjoinders to make itself translatable to its readers, to sooth and temper their a priori conception of what such a text should be. Instead, 'The House of Hunger' is in reality marked by extremes, graphic violence, and a refusal to mediate or equivocate. In narrative terms, the novella is bewildering in its temporal and spatial slippages, producing a vision which is deliberately disturbing and discomfiting, broadly realist, but hardly within the parameters of an Achebeian realism. Where in *Things Fall Apart* we see a vision of the world at the moment of colonial intrusion in which both coloniser and colonised are humanised, reflected as full, if flawed, individuals, in 'The House of Hunger' little

---

[63] Letter from James Currey to Tom Engelhardt at Pantheon books regarding the American edition of *The House of Hunger*, 30 March 1979, University of Reading Special Collections, Heinemann Educational Books, African Writers Series.

is to be grasped but the sheer 'gut rot' of a 'Kafka-esque and angst-ridden' society,[64] striated by violence and a hatred of a life in which to live is to exist, in 'that House of Hunger where every morsel of sanity was snatched from you the way some kinds of bird snatch food from the very mouths of babes'.[65]

The world of 'The House of Hunger' is mediated by the hierarchies of power and violence, removing the distinctions between life and death, humankind, and its others. This is a world in which the movement from childhood through adolescence to adulthood is not one of rites and meaning, but one of an 'emptiness [. . .] deep-seated in the gut' before which only 'lay another vast emptiness whose appetite for things living was at best wolfish' (13). A far cry from the humanistic vision of the past seen in the writing of Achebe, Ngũgĩ, and their Francophone counterparts Kane and Laye, township life in 'The House of Hunger' throbs and pulses through the seething violence at its core, its reduction of life into a negative image that does not ever quite settle into a graspable object, moving, permutating, and evolving such that form and image lose all grounding, with no possible restitution. One of the most striking aspects of 'The House of Hunger' is its refusal of an authentic or autonomous vision of African cultural production. Rather, the cultural, social, and ideological landscape of the novella is riven with multiple lineages and lines of influence which together fabricate a stark critique of the cultural nationalist vision of self-determination. In one telling scene, describing a vicious school fight, the narrative references the African Writers Series itself, its eventual home:

[64] Readers report by Henry Chakava, University of Reading Special Collections, Heinemann Educational Books, African Writers Series.

[65] Dambudzo Marechera, *The House of Hunger* (London: Heinemann Educational Books, 2009 [1978]), p. 11. All subsequent references to this edition cited in text.

The Edmund-Stephen fight was the most talked-about event the year it happened. It even outclassed Smith's UDI [Unilateral Declaration of Independence]. This is how it happened. Stephen was older, bigger and broader, than anyone else in the first form. Stephen was mean, a bully, a typical African bully in an ordinary African school. He had appropriated for his own specific use such notable figures as Nkrumah, Kaunda, Che, Castro, Stalin, Mao, Kennedy, Nyerere and, for that matter, everyone else who could be dragged into an after-hours dormitory argument. [. . .] Stephen detested 'classical' music. And for some reason Stephen thought Gogol was the one great enemy of Africa who had to be stamped out at all cost. Stephen was an avid reader of the Heinemann African Writers Series. He firmly believed that there was something peculiarly African in anything written by an African and said that therefore European tools of criticism should not be used in the analysis of 'African literature'. [. . .] (80)

Dense with intertextuality, this passage fabricates a cultural landscape and network of influence which functions as a constituent aspect of its narrative of violence and despoliation. As Quayson notes, 'the allegorical inflection of the fight is unmistakable',[66] with its references to Ian Smith's UDI eliding into its culturalist framework, what we might read as a reinsertion of politics within the seemingly disinterested world of art. Stephen, 'a typical African bully', is quickly positioned in relation to a cultural field derived from an anticolonial, pan-Africanist intellectualism, citing a veritable laundry list of foundational

[66] Ato Quayson, *Calibrations: Reading for the Social* (Minneapolis: University of Minnesota Press, 2003), p. 85.

figures in the anticolonial struggle, while simultaneously rejecting the 'classical' (or one might say 'canonical') pillars of so-called Western culture as an assertion of difference, self-determination, and autonomy. A nativist and believer in the notion of an African personality, and an 'avid reader of the Heinemann African Writers Series', Stephen emerges as a character for whom the performativity of a certain ossified image of Africanness functions as an alibi for violence, destruction, and a rigid maintenance of the social hierarchy. Following this brief passage, the narrative recounts an incident in which Stephen turns his hatred to a fellow classmate, Edmund:

> [Edmund] was on his hands and knees in a pool of blood. His face was unrecognisable. And he was whining; jabbering distractedly like an animal. I almost cried when I finally understood what it was he was saying; he was saying over and over 'I'm a monkey, I'm a baboon, I'm a monkey, I'm a baboon'. Most of his front teeth had gone and his jaw seemed to be hanging on by a thread. Great scabs of blood were forming all over his eyes, nose, mouth, and cheeks. (82)

Earlier revealed in the novella to have become a freedom fighter against the racist Smith regime, later turned into a spectacle after his capture at its hands, here, Edmund is reduced to something more animal than human, debased and degraded into a state that cannot even achieve the status of bare life, pummelled by the fists of the nativist, cultural nationalist. Freedom appears as a myth, only achievable through the basest and most degrading forms of violence and the construction of internal hierarchies based around the same binary and teleological models as that which they suppose to displace. Transforming the future freedom fighter into a monkey, a baboon – deliberate references, to be sure, to the racist rhetoric used to justify the upholding of white supremacy in Southern

Africa/Rhodesia – 'The House of Hunger' portrays violence as the only possible mode of being, not for its revolutionary ability to reconstruct the self (qua Fanon), but for its very immutability as the foundation upon which the nation – past, present, and future – exists. I certainly do not wish to suggest that Dambudzo Marechera is an unknown or outsider writer, as such; indeed, the publication of *The House of Hunger* in the African Writers Series attests to at least some level of centrality. At the same time, the man and his work remain difficult to pin down in an easy, teleological story of African literature, indicated by the range of modifiers which often accompany his name: radical, rebellious, unstable – all terms which indicate a vision rather different from the liberal view of African literature. With its range of influences spanning the sociopolitical context of white supremacy in Southern Africa to the role of the radical press in that geography, what emerges in his work are a series of connections to a longer history of struggle and violence which bears little resemblance to the accommodationist, agonistic, or compromising vision of much of the culturalist discourse which surrounds the canonisation of African literature in the global North, engaging and allowing other, potentially less visible publics, narratives, and critical encounters to emerge.

2 Contemporary Canons

On 21 March 2013, Chinua Achebe passed away in Boston, Massachusetts following a short illness. Unsurprisingly, given the man's stature as a writer, thinker, teacher, and public intellectual, Achebe's death was met with worldwide tributes, inspiring several academic conferences in his memory and public events celebrating his life and legacy. The world-spanning memorials and mourning with which Achebe's death was met indicate something rather important about the ways in which the canonisation of early African literature functioned, particularly the manner in which a certain subset of writers, usually those published in Europe and North America and usually those affiliated with large institutional apparatuses such as the African Writers Series, went on to become celebrities and spokespeople in their own right, known not only for their creative work, but for their high-profile interventions in public social and political life. In Achebe's case, the author was a prominent critic of the Nigerian government, outlining what he saw as the failures of the postcolonial state in his 1983 polemic, *The Trouble with Nigeria*. Alongside countrymen including Wole Soyinka, the author maintained a high public profile alternately as a representative of the short-lived breakaway Republic of Biafra, Nigeria, and Africa as a whole. If figures such as Achebe, Soyinka, and Ngũgĩ wa Thiong'o served both as literary representatives of the continent and sociopolitical spokesmen for its emergence into the postindependence era and beyond, the elevation of the writer as media celebrity and spokesperson has only intensified in the contemporary era, amplified by the development of the Internet and digital technologies and, particularly, the rise of social media. I have written elsewhere on the role of social media in the ascendency of a 'new' canon of African writing.[67] Here, it suffices to note at the outset the particularly pernicious ways in which contemporary authors have become – through the circulation of social media, TED talks, think pieces, and viral videos – representatives and spokespeople for a certain vision of contemporary Africa which functions in an uneasy and at times agonistic relationship with the continent's larger positioning within a late capitalist global market increasingly defined by the neoliberal turn and its marketisation of everyday life.

---

[67] Madhu Krishnan, 'Periodizing the Anglophone African Novel: Location(s) in a Transnational Literary Marketplace', in *Literature and the Global Contemporary*, ed. by Sarah Brouillette, Mathias Nilges, and Emilio Sauri (Basingstoke: Palgrave Macmillan, 2017), pp. 135–56.

In Section 2, I explore the ways in which the patterns and structures of canonisation which I introduced in Section 1 have shifted in the contemporary era, defined broadly as the years which followed the neoliberal turn of the 1980s and 1990s. While hesitant to use a term whose meaning has so often been diluted such as to render it largely meaningless, my use of the term neoliberal here is intended to signal the encroachment of market principles into every part of life, characterised by financialisation, privatisation, the rise of the citizen-as-consumer, and the erosion of the public. Neoliberalism, in this view, cannot be seen as a static concept; originally an economic concept deployed in the 1970s and 1980s, it has subsequently transformed into a political mode, a sociocultural model, and finally, an ontology unto itself,[68] with a significant impact on the shaping of the literary field, both in terms of its market parameters and its work of valuation. As Mbembe highlights:

> the neoliberal drive to privatise all forms of art has resulted in the endless commodification of culture and its permanent translation into spectacle, leisure and entertainment. This significant development comes at a time when global capitalism itself is moving into a phase in which the cultural forms of its outputs are critical elements of productive strategies (Scott 2000). Because arts and culture have become an integral part of the economic, their capacity to engage critically with the velocities of capital can no

---

[68] Mitchum Huehls and Rachel Greenwald Smith, 'Four Phases of Neoliberalism and Literature: An Introduction', in *Neoliberalism and Contemporary Literary Culture*, ed. by Mitchum Huehls and Rachel Greenwald Smith (Baltimore: Johns Hopkins University Press, 2017), pp. 1–20 (p. 3).

longer be taken for granted. Spaces of culture are no longer just aesthetic spaces. They are also commercial spaces.[69]

My interest here is both to look at the larger historical continuities in the way in which African literature, as a global market category, has continued to come into being in the world while simultaneously foregrounding the particularities which drive the twinned processes of canonisation and consecration in the contemporary era. While many of the patterns and ideological discourses undergirding this process might be read through a form of continuity from previous instantiations of African literature in the global marketplace, that is, I wish to foreground how these structures and discourses have been amplified and transformed under the auspices of liquid modernity.[70]

At its core a fundamental deterritorialisation of power based on individualisation and privatisation, liquid modernity differentiates between the extraterritorial elite who rule and the settled majority, unable to reap its benefits,[71] fragmenting populations, undoing historical sites of cooperation, and leaving little left but a vacuous notion of identity equated with consumer choice. With clear implications for the spread of neoliberal discourses and practices across the globe, often moving from the new centres of power through the rest of the world in patterns which are diffuse, irregular, and idiosyncratic,[72]

---

[69] Achille Mbembe, 'At the Centre of the Knot', *Social Dynamics*, 38.1 (2012), 8–14 (p. 11).

[70] Zygmunt Bauman, *Liquid Modernity* (Cambridge: Polity Press, 2012 [2000]).

[71] Bauman, p. 13.

[72] Ferguson, for instance, notes the ways in which contemporary Africa might be defined by a series of enclave economies, functioning under the governance of nonstatist, often multinational, control, and virtual a-national deserts beyond. See James Ferguson, *Global Shadows: Africa in the Neoliberal World Order* (Durham: Duke University Press, 2006).

the era of fluidity has implied a detachment of the self from the physical and ideological institutions of community which once defined social living, moving from a focus on the collective and the structural to the individual and the affective/psychological. Along with the emerging economies of Latin America, few geographies have been reshaped to the extent that one encounters on the African continent. Seen most aptly in the spread of Bretton Woods-inflected structural adjustment programmes in the 1980s, this reshaping of the continent has taken on a number of distinctive features, notably around the erosion of public space; the privatisation of previously public goods including healthcare and education; and the opening of once-nationalised industries and resource areas to predatory market policies.[73] Notably, the entrenchment of neoliberal financialisation and free-market policies has coincided with the stagnation of national governance across the continent, evidenced in the proliferation of dictatorial practices, a correlation which coheres with Huehl and Greenwald Smith's observation that, in its second stage from roughly the Reagan/Thatcher era, neoliberalism appears as a mode of political governance.[74]

Unsurprisingly, for many commentators of African literature this period was accompanied by something of a slump in the field, marked on the one hand by the so-called African book famine and, on the other, by the constriction of reading cultures as access to education was gradually closed off to large masses

---

[73] See Patrick Bond, *Looting Africa: The Economics of Exploitation* (London: Zed Books, 2006); Tom Burgis, *The Looting Machine: Warlords, Tycoons, Smugglers and the Systematic Theft of Africa's Wealth* (London: HarperCollins, 2015); Pádraig Carmody, *The New Scramble for Africa* (Cambridge: Polity Press, 2011); Ian Taylor, *Africa Rising? BRICS – Diversifying Dependency* (Woodbridge: Boydell & Brewer, 2014).

[74] Huehls and Greenwald Smith, pp. 6–7.

of the population.[75] As Emma Shercliff notes, until the institution of the African Books Collective in the 1990s, African publishing was severely hampered by the domination of the multinational publishers in the lucrative educational and textbook sector, arguing that 'the exclusion of local commercial publishers and booksellers from the lucrative school market until the liberalisation of textbook provision in the 1990s resulted in a lack of investment in the industry and a legacy of inefficiency, low quality and corruption within the African state publishing monopolies',[76] an observation repeated elsewhere.[77] The notion that African literature went into something of a dormant period in this time is not, of course, to say that African literary production, in its fuller sense, did. Indeed, the 1980s and early 1990s were years in which many areas of literary production on the continent flourished, particularly around women's writing. Yet, in the story of its canonisation, there appears to be a clear correlation between the era of political neoliberalism and a virtual disappearance of African literature from the front lines of the global literary market, due largely to the dearth of outlets for writers based on the continent. The reemergence of African literature on a world stage, then, might be seen as most closely linked with the development of neoliberalism into a sociocultural formation and, most recently, as an ontological framework for understanding the self and the world,[78] a shift which coincides roughly with the rise of a particular set of African literary stars in the global North and an attendant opening of the publishing market on the continent. Where African literature, in particular, might once have been

---

[75] See Hans Zell, 'Publishing in Africa', in *International Book Publishing: An Encyclopedia*. ed. by P. G. Altbach and E. S. Hoshino (New York: Garland Publishing, 1995), pp. 366–73.

[76] Emma Shercliff, 'African Publishing in the Twenty-First Century', *Wasafiri*, 31.4 (2016) 10–12 (p. 10).

[77] Nathalie Carré, 'From Local to Global', *Wasafiri*, 31.4 (2016) 56–62 (p. 57).

[78] Huehls and Greenwald Smith, pp. 9–10.

read through the ethnographic and anthropological lens, as a means of deci-
phering these 'other' cultures, or, more starkly, in Huggan's terms, as a mode of
mastery, the canonisation of contemporary African literature appears to point
to a new pattern emerging, one in which the rise of the autonomous individual,
unmoored from the pesky business of politics and economics, has come to the
fore and one which, not without coincidence, aligns to the dominant reading of
the Afropolitan ideal of the mobile subject, which I discuss below.

Contemporary criticism, like its predecessors, has revolved around
a limited set of debates which implicitly and explicitly shape the reading
practices which shape the contours of African literature today: the castigation
of what is called poverty porn in representations of the continent;[79] recurrent
arguments around the global aesthetics of the extroverted African novel
versus multifocal readings;[80] debates around the location of African literature
and the status of diasporic or migrant literature therein. My discussion in this
section, however, will focus on what has become the critical paradigm
par excellence against which African literature has been shaped in its contemporary guise, Afropolitanism. Despite its relative theoretical thinness as a

---

[79] Helon Habila, 'We Need New Names by NoViolet Bulawayo – review', *Guardian*,
20 June 2013, www.theguardian.com/books/2013/jun/20/need-new-names-bula
wayo-review, accessed 29 January 2018.

[80] Akin Adesokan, *Postcolonial Artists and Global Aesthetics* (Bloomington: Indiana
University Press, 2011); Eileen Julien, 'The Extroverted African Novel', in
The Novel: History, Geography and Culture. Vol 1, ed. Franco Moretti (Princeton:
Princeton University Press, 2006), pp. 667–700; Nathan Suhr-Sytsma,
'The Extroverted African Novel and Literary Publishing in the Twenty-First
Century', *Journal of African Cultural Studies*, www.tandfonline.com/doi/abs/
10.1080/13696815.2017.1400953, accessed 29 January 2018.

concept,[81] Afropolitanism, now the subject of countless think pieces, journal articles, special issues, edited collections and more,[82] has become something of a compulsory grounding point against which the contours of African literature are measured. Variously attributed, the concept of the Afropolitan first entered the Anglophone critical sphere following the publication in 2005 of a short piece titled 'Bye-Bye Babar' by writer Taiye Selasi. Describing the Afropolitan as marked by 'our funny blend of London fashion, New York jargon, African ethics, and academic successes', having 'at least one place on The African Continent to which we tie our sense of self: be it a nation-state (Ethiopia), a city (Ibadan), or an auntie's kitchen' and 'the G8 city or two (or three) that we know like the backs of our hands',[83] the Afropolitan, according to this understanding, functions as the ideal subject of the neoliberal turn. Defined by liquidity, the Afropolitan may badge themselves as a citizen of the world, but their daily movements and self-conception remain contingent on their admission to a global system structured around the deterritorialisation of capital. This, in turn, gives the Afropolitan access to a privileged world of flows, beneficiary of a life imbued with what appears to be endless mobility and the freedom of choice to define one's identity at will. Adopting and

[81] Anna-Leena Toivanen, 'Cosmopolitanism's New Clothes? The Limits of the Concept of Afropolitanism', *European Journal of English Studies*, 21.2 (2017) 189–205 (p. 190).

[82] Recent special issues and volumes include *European Journal of English Studies*, 21.2 (2017); *Journal of African Cultural Studies*, 28:1 (2016); Eva Rask Knudsen and Ulla Rahbek, *In Search of the Afropolitan* (London: Rowman and Littlefield, 2016); Jennifer Wawrzinek and J. K. S. Makokha (eds), *Negotiating Afropolitanism: Essays on Borders and Spaces in Contemporary African Literature and Folklore* (Amsterdam: Rodopi, 2011).

[83] Taiye Selasi, 'Bye-Bye Babar', *The LIP Magazine*, 3 March 2005, www.thelip.robert sharp.co.uk/?p=76, accessed 29 January 2018.

discarding identities in the name of liquidity, this reading of Afropolitanism transforms the act of being into another marketplace transaction, mediated by commoditisation like any other.

This formulation of Afropolitanism has engendered no shortage of critical responses, ranging from those which laud the potential therein 'to cross the psychic boundaries erected by nativism, autochthony, heritage, and other mythologies of authenticity',[84] on the one hand, and those which castigate the concept as simply another means through which the very hierarchies and structures undergirding the capitalist-colonialist exploitation of the African continent proliferate.[85] Yet, as Bosch Santana notes, much of the discussion in the Anglophone critical sphere around Afropolitanism forgets that the term derives not from Selasi's essay, in its first instance, but rather from a longer series of philosophical debates, led notably by Achille Mbembe.[86] For Mbembe, Afropolitanism is no new phenomenon, but rather describes the historical condition of the continent as a place of crossings, entanglements, mixing, and *métissage*, 'refer[ring] to a way – the many ways – in which Africans, or people of African origin, understand themselves as being part of the world rather than being apart', in a direct challenge to the Hegelian vision of the continent as outside of the world and history. Afropolitanism, then, 'is a name for undertaking a critical reflection on the many ways in which, in fact, there is

---

[84] Chielozona Eze, 'We, Afropolitans', *Journal of African Cultural Studies*, 28.1 (2016), 114–19.

[85] Emma Dabiri, 'Why I Am (Still) Not an Afropolitan', *Journal of African Cultural Studies*, 28.1 (2016), 104–8; Grace A. Musila, 'Part-Time Africans, Europolitans and "Africa Lite"', *Journal of African Cultural Studies*, 28.1 (2016), 109–13.

[86] As Bosch Santana notes, one reason for the relative neglect of Mbembe's account is that, appearing in *La Grande Sortie de la Nuit*, it has not yet been translated into English. See Stephanie Bosch Santana, 'Exorcizing the Future: Afropolitanism's Spectral Origins', *Journal of African Cultural Studies*, 28.1 (2016) 120–6.

no world without Africa and there is no Africa that is not part of it'.[87] Afropolitanism thus functions as a mode of decentring, enabling a multiple vision of the continent unmoored from the chains of authenticity or static notions of tradition, foregrounding the long durée of entanglements which have defined both the ways in which Africa has been worlded and has itself enacting a form of worlding, in the broad sense.

Despite the complexity of Mbembe's account, however, there remain aspects of it which, when applied to the contemporary literary field, remain problematic. Central to Mbembe's account is a desire to move away from the racialised, essentialist vision of the African continent. This is certainly a goal with much merit; at the same time, it lends itself to the sense that the turn to Afropolitanism functions as a premature synthesis to a dialectical movement which has not completed its first two turns, making cosmopolitan, without structurally reconstituting that which has historically been overdetermined by racialised discourse, African literature. Further still, the subtler account of Afropolitanism constructed in Mbembe's arguments has occupied far less attention within the popular imagination than the pithy and consumerist vision produced by Selasi, the latter according much more strongly with the contours of contemporary African literature in its market form than the former. In many ways, it might seem that the new canon of African literature is indeed Afropolitan, with the names appearing most frequently in its ranks attached to mobile, diasporic, and multirooted individuals who seem, on the surface, to embody the ethos of privileged mobility and individualism which the term entails. Among authors, of course, there is no consensus on the relative value of the term, and many – Chimamanda Ngozi Adichie and Binyavanga Wainaina,

---

[87] Sarah Balakrishnan, 'Pan-African Legacies, Afropolitan Futures: A Conversation with Achille Mbembe', *Transition*, 120 (2016), 28–37 (p. 29).

for instance – have explicitly rejected the term.[88] Yet, Afropolitanism repeats itself time and again as a buzzword or marketing label. The anxieties which underwrite much of the critical debate around the term can be seen as part of a longer history of anxiety around the question of representation in African literature, and particularly the impact of the politics of location with respect to readers, writers, producers, and gatekeepers. Implicit here is the constant notion of the dual mandate, that which imbues the literary with a meaning which is never simply about the literary, but rather about larger questions of the continent's place in the world and its image therein.

Much of the critical debate around Afropolitanism has occurred not in the hallowed pages of academic journals, but on the relatively open spaces of the Internet. The rise of social media and blogs as primary platforms through which literary activity is mediated serves as a central driver in the canon formation practices which mediate the contours of contemporary African literature. Equally as significant has been the role of digital media in consecrating the role of spokesperson or media star for certain African writers themselves. In Section 1, I argued that the constitution and canonisation of African literature, at least in the story most visible in the global literary field, has always relied on a series of totemic figures and mythical moments/ founding moments. In the contemporary era, with the omnipresence of digital technologies, the hyperactive space-time compression of blogs, podcasting, and vodcasting, and the immediacy of social media, the role of the writer-as-star has intensified, amplifying the anxieties, tensions, and ambiguities which attend the dual mandate of the writer as artist and writer as spokesperson. Evident in the contemporary landscape, that is, are what function essentially

---

[88] Adichie has famously referred to herself as a 'happy African' and Wainaina a pan-Africanist.

as cults of personality, enabled by the speed and spread of digital technologies to proliferate and continually reproduce their own rhetoric to the benefit of a select group of writers with the savvy to manipulate the possibilities of digital space for publicity and amplification. The overall effect of these echo chambers has been, despite the allegedly democratising potential of digital communications, to reduce, concentrate, and encircle the spaces possible for discourse discussion and debate, consecrating a small and elite group of writers as social media stars. Unsurprisingly, these writers, including Adichie, Teju Cole, Francophone Congolese writer Alain Mabankcou (not coincidentally, one of the few Francophone writers to make it into the consecrated field of literary stars), are all attached in various ways to major metropolitan publishing houses and other outlets; relatively little space is given, on the other hand, to those works and authors attached to lesser-known institutions, despite the existence of platforms engaged in discussion therein.

Teju Cole's 2011 novel *Open City* has in many ways become the paradigmatic exemplar of this new vision of African literature. Deeply poetic in its register, the novel is a philosophical meditation on history, culture, and society, told from the perspective of its first-person narrator, Julius, a Nigerian-German psychiatry fellow living in New York City. Organised around a series of long nocturnal walks and loose encounters with a wide and diverse cast of characters, *Open City* has been variously compared to the writings of W. G. Sebald, Baudelaire, and others, lauded for its presentation of the African-immigrant flâneur. In a 2016 essay, Chielozona Eze makes an explicit connection between Julius and the ideal Afropolitan:

> Julius the protagonist stands out for his openness to the world. Characteristic of his relation to New York is his mobility. [. . .]

> This mobility is richly symbolic of his self-perception as
> a global citizen and a person with an open mind.[89]

Against this reading, I have written extensively about the ways in which the novel's constitution of neoliberal spatiality functions at odds with its ostensibly disinterested cosmopolitan engagements,[90] and I will not repeat these arguments here. Instead, my focus in this brief discussion focuses on the cultural landscape which the novel develops and its ostensible play with notions of fluidity, interconnectedness, and politics in the contemporary era. The novel repeatedly foregrounds Julius's consumption of culture as a critical aspect of his engagement with and in the world, emphasised in its early pages, where the narrator recounts his habit of listening to European radio stations, describing how he 'liked the murmur of the announcers, the sounds of those voices speaking calmly from thousands of miles away',[91] integrating them into his evening rituals:

> When it became dark, I would pick up a book and read by the
> light of an old desk lamp I had rescued from one of the
> dumpsters at the university; its bulb was hooded by a glass
> bell that cast a greenish light over my hands, the book on my
> lap, the worn upholstery of the sofa. Sometimes, I even spoke
> the words in the book out loud to myself, and doing so I noticed
> the odd way my voice mingled with the murmur of the French,

---

[89] Eze, p. 115.

[90] Madhu Krishnan, 'Postcoloniality, Spatiality and Cosmopolitanism in the Open City', *Textual Practice*, 29.4 (2015), 675–96.

[91] Teju Cole, *Open City* (London: Faber and Faber, 2011), p. 4. Subsequent references to this edition are cited in the text.

> German, or Dutch radio announcers, or with the thin texture of
> the violin strings of the orchestras, all of this intensified by the
> fact that whatever it was I was reading had likely been translated
> out of one of the European languages. That fall, I flitted from
> book to book: Barthes's *Cameria Lucida*, Peter Altenberg's
> *Telegrams of the Soul*, Tahar Ben Jellouns's *The Last Friend*,
> among others. (5)

At a superficial level, the cultural field forged in this passage reinforces the
reading of Julius as consummate global citizen, able to merge idioms, histories,
and cultural landscapes into a seamless and holistic totality through his studied
consumption. Across the novel, cultural consumption acts as one of the primary
modes of characterisation, creating a narrative frame in which Julius himself
becomes metonymically represented by these various examples of high art,
their cultural capital, prestige, and resonance standing in for his own personality, otherwise left deliberately vacuous, producing a sense that it is only
through art that Julius can come to know the world around him and become an
agent or actor in said world. Indeed, in many ways Julius's own narration
underscores this point, dwelling upon and ruminating on the power of culture
to move, to shape, and to transform.

Yet, this reading of the novel sits uneasily with its larger narratorial
force; despite his affinity for high culture Julius remains a solipsistic character,
unknowable and unable to connect in any meaningful way with his many
interlocutors and encounters, his discomfited anger clear when a taxi driver
hails him as his brother (40); bewildered by the news, several months belatedly,
that one of his neighbours had died without his noticing or realising (20–1); and
uninformed of the death of his former professor and mentor (183–4). Indeed,
even that the one person with whom Julius retains some repeated contact in the
novel is known only as '[his] friend' is significant, evacuating all content and

personality other than Julius's own. Throughout his encounters, Julius remains a flat character, seemingly unchanged and unchangeable, viewing the world through a lens of equivalence and exchangeability in which little appears to matter in and of itself. Emphasised by a circular, largely episodic structure, beginning and ending in the same place, with Julius's musing on bird migrations, *Open City* produces a sense of stasis barely marked over by its superficial fluidity. It is this very attitude which is parodied in Cole's 2014 essay, 'What It Is', originally published in *the New Yorker*.[92] Inspired by a CNN headline which asked 'Ebola: "The ISIS of biological agents?"', the essay begins by asking, 'Is Ebola the ISIS of biological agents? Is Ebola the Boko Haram of AIDS? Is Ebola the al-Shabaab of dengue fever?'. Running through an increasingly frenetic list of equivalences and analogies parodying the hackneyed attempt to decipher through equivalence, the essay mocks the reductive rhetorical techniques which characterise the neoliberal turn, in which everything and anything can only exist as an exchangeable – and therefore somehow equivalent – commodity. This is a mode of being in which little counts but the exchange value inhered to a person, place, or thing, mediated by its distribution along an uneven North/South axis that cannibalises the different, the particular, and the singular into a bland formation of the same.

In *Open City*'s climactic scene, standing on a balcony overlooking the Hudson River and the great expanse of Manhattan, Julius is confronted by Moji, a former friend from Nigeria now also in New York City, forced to reckon her revelation that as a teenager he had raped her, an incident of which he purports no memory. Despite his ostensible shock at discovering that in Moji's story he is the villain, this realisation, too, effects little change in either Julius or the narrative voice more broadly, eventually returning to where it

[92] Teju Cole, 'What It Is', *New Yorker*, 7 October 2014, www.newyorker.com/books/page-turner/what-is-ebola, accessed 29 January 2018.

began. The novel thus leverages its radically unreliable narration to develop a chasm between the easy consumption of culture, ostensibly a mode of world formation and means through which to develop one's human capital, and an actual mode of living in the world, with others, under the precepts of an ethical-political mode of being. It is of no small consequence, then, that for all of his musings and meanderings, including those ostensibly engaged moments at the site of the former World Trade Centre, American Folk Art Museum, and elsewhere, Julius remains a starkly apolitical character, individualistic to his core, unmoored from the bonds of family, society, and nation, and, as we discover in this scene, utterly mired in a form of narcissism which blinds him to structures of violence which undergird his seemingly apolitical life in a manner which seems, ironically, to mimic the cosmopolitan reading of the novel itself.

No contemporary author has become as representative of African literature as Chimamanda Ngozi Adichie. Adichie's rise to superstardom is remarkable; in addition to the many prizes and acclaim garnered by her work, Adichie has also been recipient of the MacArthur grant, often called the 'genius grant'; gone viral twice over, first with her 2008 TED talk, 'The Danger of a Single Story', and then again in 2014 when another TED talk, 'We Should All Be Feminists', was sampled in Beyoncé's single 'Flawless'; earned sponsorships including a high-profile role as the new face of No.7, the in-house cosmetics brand of UK pharmacy chain Boots; and countless appearances on television, radio, and the Internet across the world as a public intellectual and global spokeswoman for African feminism and contemporary affairs. Photogenic, fashionable, and erudite, raised in a home once owned by Achebe, Adichie, in her public guise, comes across as a master of the mythologies which surround African literature. At the same time, it would be patently false to suggest that Adichie is merely another postcolonial writer operating under the sway of the global literary market and its whims. In addition to expanding the imaginative horizons which delineate the contours of Africa in a global imaginary through her focus on middle-class, intellectual, and family life, Adichie herself occupies a more complex position within the global literary field. As Kate Haines Wallis has deftly illustrated, Adichie's activities, taken as a whole, demonstrate the existence of alternative literary geographies based on flows and networks of intimacy which are simultaneously pan-African in their purview and in dialogue with elsewhere,[93] notably through the reprinting of her major works through Farafina Press, a Nigeria-based publishing company and one-time magazine, and her institution of the Farafina Creative Writing Workshop, aimed at continental writers with the purpose of 'giv[ing them] the opportunity to be part of an engaged community of writers and readers',[94] and serving as an important part in the struggle to redistribute cultural and intellectual capital from the global North to the South.

At the same time, the reception and consecration of Adichie's work indicates the extent to which the processes of canonisation that determine the contours of contemporary African literature overdetermine a set of parameters based on the precepts of fluidity, neoliberal individualism, and the transformation of politics into culture. If the story of the institution of African literature suggests that prior to Achebe all that existed was an expectant pause, then with Adichie one might be tempted to perceive a long-deferred moment of exhalation, the messianic conclusion of a decades-long story, seeing African literature to the glorious final act of its teleological development at last. A brief look at the author's institutional consecration underscores this point: in the previous three years, for instance, the African Literature Association's annual conference has seen a minimum

---

[93] Kate Haines Wallis, 'Exchanges in Nairobi and Lagos: Literary Networks as Alternative Geographies', *Research in African Literatures*, 49.1 (2018), 163–186.

[94] Farafina Trust, www.farafinatrust.org/, accessed 29 January 2018.

of two panels dedicated solely to Adichie's work (far more than any other contemporary writer), with dozens of additional papers delivered on panels elsewhere per year; a search for criticism on the Modern Language Association International Bibliography, the largest single index of published peer-reviewed research in the humanities, meanwhile, brings up 189 results, a partial metric but one which is astonishing nonetheless (by comparison, searches for criticism on Teju Cole produced 41 results; Binyavanga Wainaina 16; Sefi Atta 32; Alain Mabanckou 96; Helon Habila 32; Yewande Omotose 1; and Chris Abani 94). Adichie's own comments support this vision of the author as the centre of the contemporary literary field, most notably in her response, when asked by a reviewer about the importance of the Caine Prize for African Writing, that she needn't bother with such things as all of the best fiction from Africa come straight to her inbox.[95]

I wish to turn briefly now to Adichie's most recent full-length novel, *Americanah* (2013). In many ways, *Americanah* is nothing less than a story about fluidity and mobility, in all of its senses. The novel centres largely on Ifemula, a young woman from humble middle-class origins, who is repeatedly characterised by her singularity among her peers and her uniquely expressive disposition to the world. Across the narrative, Ifemula moves from her home city of Lagos to the United States on a university scholarship, where, following a brief period of financial hardship that includes a single foray into sex work and subsequent crippling depression, she eventually finds herself in a position of relative wealth and fame as the force behind a popular blog. So popular is the blog that it enables her to land a prestigious fellowship at Princeton University.

[95] Aaron Bady, 'The Varieties of Blackness: An Interview with Chimamanda Ngozi Adichie', *The Boston Review*, www.bostonreview.net/fiction/varieties-blackness, accessed 29 January 2018. The interview subsequently led to controversy when Adichie referred to the Farafina workshop participants as 'her boys'.

Despite her affluent and charmed life (unsurprisingly, Ifemula is also described as the object of desire in two long-term relationships with wealthy, handsome, and impossibly devoted American men, one white and one black), Ifemula eventually returns to her home city of Lagos, where she reunites (with some bumps along the way, not the least of which is the pesky existence of a loving wife) with Obzine, 'her first love, her first lover, the only person with whom she had never felt the need to explain herself'.[96] As this brief and partial plot summary suggests (along with Ifemula's story is the less-developed parallel story of Obinze, her one-time lover, whose own trajectory includes a stint as an undocumented worker in the United Kingdom, deportation, and an uncommon success at the hustle of Nigerian social life), *Americanah* has been largely received as an exemplar of contemporary literary fiction,[97] chronicling the struggles which accompany middle-class mobility and forging a vision of the world of flows which does not depend upon the diminishment of roots.

For all of the extent to which it has been positioned as an exemplary text of mobility and cosmopolitan fluidity, however, *Americanah* remains ambivalent. Ifemula, despite the novel's insistence on her unique presence and startling beauty, presents as a character with little substance. Early in the novel's pages she is described as enjoying her life in Princeton precisely because of its lack of smell, of presence, and how it allowed her to 'pretend to be someone else, someone specially admitted into a hallowed American club, someone adorned with certainty' (3); elsewhere, recounting her nervous teenaged preparations for her first meeting with Obinze's mother, the narrative describes her bewilderment at her aunt's advice that she just be herself, to which she can only

---

[96] Chimamanda Ngozi Adichie, *Americanah* (London: Fourth Estate, 2013), p. 6. Subsequent references to this edition are cited in the text.

[97] The reception of *Americanah* as literary fiction is itself a point for debate, given that the novel broadly conforms to the conventions of chick lit and other genre fiction.

wonder 'What does that even mean?' (68). Despite her eventual prosperity in America, Ifemelu is described in a manner far from the happy connectivity of Selasi's Afropolitan, plagued instead by a heaviness described like having 'cement in her soul' (6) and 'an early morning disease of fatigue, a bleakness and borderlessness. It brought with it amorphous longings, shapeless desires, brief imaginary glints of other lives she could be living, that over the months melded into a piercing homesickness' (6). The only tonic to this emptiness, we learn, are Ifemelu's dreams of a return to Lagos, her obsessive scouring of the Internet for stories of returnees, and her bitterness at the realisation that they were 'living her life' (6), the life intended for her. Rather than propose a view of the world in which places and spaces contain some fundamental exchangeability as objects of consumption contained and connected by flows and sharing a larger humanistic commonality, *Americanah* constitutes a spatial frame in which places remain distinct, captured in Ifemula's savage mockery of the Lagos-based Nigeropolitan club and its complaints – complaints which she, too, participates in – that Lagos should be more like New York (421).

Throughout the novel, connection and connectivity, for Ifemula, remain difficult to achieve: in one brief scene, Ifemula's relief at finding her university's African students' association is described as 'a gentle, swaying sense of renewal', a release from the imperative to always explain oneself (139), only to dissipate into the background, abandoned as Ifemula enters into a relationship with Curt, the wealthy cousin of her employer, who seamlessly integrates her into his white world:

> That was what Curt had given her, this gift of contentment, of ease. How quickly she had become used to their life, her passport filled with visa stamps, the solicitousness of flight attendants in first-class cabins, the feathery bed linen in the hotels they stayed in and the little things she hoarded: jars of preserves

from the breakfast tray, little vials of conditioners, woven
slippers, even face towels if they were especially soft. She had
slipped out of her old skin. (200)

In this moment, Ifemula seems, at last, to have escaped the empty longing that
dictated her life before, a life filled by the desperate desire 'to be from the
country of people who gave and not those who received, to be one of those who
had and could therefore bask in the grace of having given, to be among those
who could afford copious pity and empathy' (170), to bathe in the affluence of
connectivity. And yet, the narrative quickly reveals this to be but another brief
and fragmentary moment, as fleeting as the relationship upon which it was
based, leaving Ifemula again stranded, alone and empty.

For Ifemula, then, the only real sense of connection or fullness occurs
when she starts her blog, an anonymous take on race in America titled
*Raceteenth Or Various Observations About American Blacks (Those Formerly
Known as Negroes) by a Non-American Black* (later to be replaced, after her
return to Lagos, with a new blog, *Small Redemptions of Lagos*), a process
described as exhilarating and frightening, marked by her obsession with
posted comments, the influx of speaker's fees, workshop invitations, and
media appearances which transform her from Ifemula into simply 'the
Blogger', in some way transfigured (306). And yet, the blog, too, remains
superficial: as she complains to a later boyfriend, Blaine, a young African-
American assistant professor and political activist, the purpose of the blog is
not to explain or act, but merely to observe (312), her musings on race
transformed from political interventions into cultural commentary and enter-
tainment. The blog, too, becomes another manifestation in the text of the
solipsism which defines Ifemula's characterisation. Entering into conversations with strangers not to connect but rather 'to see if [they] would say
something she could use in her blog' (4), 'sit[ting] in cafes, or airports, or train

stations, watching strangers, imagining their lives, and wondering which of them were likely to have read her blog' (5), Ifemula is again described as vacuous at her core, the deeper structures of her characterisation subverting and refuting the novel's overarching cosmopolitan, mobile guise. Repeatedly castigated by her friends for her judgemental attitude (419, 422), Ifemula's narrative trajectory fabricates a character who effectively erases all that she is meant to embody.

Americanah was released to generally positive reviews in the American and British presses: the *New York Times*, for instance, insists that the novel 'never feels false',[98] while the *Guardian* refers to it as a novel which both 'tell[s] a great story and [. . .] make[s] you change the way you look at the world.'[99] At the time of writing, the novel holds a rating of 4.3/5 based on 148,524 ratings on popular book review site Goodreads and an Amazon.com score of 4.5/5 based on 3,756 reviews. South Africa-based Chimurenga's *Chronic Books Supplement*, by contrast (a publication about which I will have more to say in Section 3) provides another perspective to the novel, beginning with an astute observation about Adichie the brand: 'For the Western, liberal world, there is no doubting the uniqueness, the intelligence and the power of this woman of letters. But her positioning is the real crux of the matter: Adichie has swum the undercurrents

---

[98] Mike Peed, 'Realities of Race', *New York Times*, 7 June 2013, www.nytimes.com/2013/06/09/books/review/americanah-by-chimamanda-ngozi-adichie.html, accessed 29 January 2018. It is worth noting that another review in that same publication, while generally positive, is less warm: Janet Maslin, 'Braiding Hair and Issues About Race', *New York Times*, 19 May 2013, www.nytimes.com/2013/05/20/books/americanha-by-chimamanda-ngozi-adichie.html, accessed 29 January 2018.

[99] Elizabeth Day, 'Americanah by Chimamanda Ngozi Adichie – review', *Guardian*, 15 April 2013, www.theguardian.com/books/2013/apr/15/americanah-chimamanda-ngozi-adichie-review, accessed 29 January 2018.

of *Americanah* and she is invested in every nuance.'[100] The review goes on to cite the relatively underdeveloped narrative style of the text, its force more 'than a suggestion, a sermon';[101] castigates Ifemula as a 'tiresome protagonist' whose characterisation suffers because 'she is too invested in Adichie's agenda';[102] characterises it as a narrative based on telling rather than showing, beating its readers with its own message such that '[w]e are offered this hostility, this standing apart in rooms and deciding what boxes people fall into, as strength or acute intelligence or Nigerian Phillip Roth';[103] and notes the extent to which the narrative is permeated by 'the familiar, low-key whine that feels almost obligatory to the process and the integrity of writing about Nigeria', evidenced 'in the references to the usual suspects of 419 pastors, university lecturers' strikes and corruption'.[104] At its core, the review complains that *Americanah* suffers because 'Adichie has got the shape of the Nigerian world wrong. She has also underestimated its size and its complexity. Africa is immeasurable. It is a living, muscular bricolage flexing and expanding backward and forward through all the manifestations of time and space'.[105] It is by no means unusual for a text which is largely well-received to be the object of one or two outlier reviews. However, I have dwelled for some time on the *Chronic Books Supplement* review because of what it might tell us about the forms of critical discourse and positioning which function differently across location, gesturing again to the twinned questions of canon formation and visibility as iterative processes. In the case of the *Chronic Books Supplement* review, what we find is a mode of reception which filters through the landscape of public debate and creativity centred on the African continent, and not through a hazy vision of Africa, the exotic unknown-known, mediated by the telegenic figure of the

---

[100] Yemisi Ogbe, 'Americanah and Other Definitions of Supple Citizenship', *Chronic Books Supplement*, August 2013, pp. 8–11 (p. 10).

[101] Ogbe, p. 10. [102] Ogbe, p. 10. [103] Ogbe, p. 10. [104] Ogbe, p. 11. [105] Ogbe, p. 11.

naïve informant-cum-public intellectual. That such a reading might be more sceptical to the novel's neoliberal claims towards individuality and human capital, moreover, calibrates with the lived manifestations of neoliberal policy in places like South Africa, a geography in which the hallowed promises of liquid modernity and the fluidity of the contemporary might perhaps ring more hollowly than the vaunted centres of the global North.

It has always been the case that any particular canon of literature can be distilled to a set of representative figures (one might consider, for instance, the continued puissance of figures like Shakespeare, Eliot, and Dickens within the canon of British literature). At the same time, there is something particular at play in the African context, what in Section 1 I discussed as the fundamental emptiness and authority with which the continent is received. Here, I wish to return to Mbembe and his excavation of this phenomenon, one which, in his reading, has historically accompanied outside perceptions, fantasies, and imaginations of the African continent. In *Critique of Black Reason*, Mbembe argues that

> For a long time, in the Western imagination, Africa was an unknown land. But that hardly prevented philosophers, naturalists, geographers, missionaries, writers, or really anyone at all from making pronouncements about one or another aspect of its geography, or about the lives, habits, and customs of its inhabitants. *Despite the flood of information to which we now have access and the number of academic studies at our disposal, it remains unclear whether the will to ignorance has disappeared*, not to mention the age-old disposition that consists in making pronouncements on subjects about which one knows little or nothing.[106]

---

[106] Mbembe, *Critique*, p. 70, emphasis added.

Shaped by a centuries-long historical trajectory beginning in the fifteenth century, with the institution of the Atlantic slave trade, and continuing to the present-day era of humanitarian 'intervention', resource exploitation, and neoliberal policy, Africa, Mbembe argues, has been subject to a curious doubling in which it is both that geography about which almost nothing is known – or can be known – and simultaneously that geography only knowable through the interlocution of the global North and its band of ignorant experts, 'a geographic location and a region of the world about which almost nothing is known but which is described with an apparent authority, the authority of fiction'.[107] I believe that Mbembe's choice of words here, emphasising the 'authority of fiction', are no mere rhetorical gloss.[108] Rather, these comments speak directly to the ways in which fictional renderings of the continent have always shaped and continue to shape the ways in which it is viewed outside of its boundaries. In the case of African literature since Achebe, it is this simultaneous ignorance and authority which has enabled certain figures and texts to be positioned not merely as one story about the continent, but the only story or the only story worth reading. And here, it is no coincidence that in the contemporary era the stories so elevated are those which remain untainted by the spectre of politics, institutions, or the structural conditions under which violence, inequity, and injustice continue to proliferate, hastening the acceleration of global inequality in an ostensible era of connection and mobility.

In this sense, both *Americanah* and *Open City* are exemplars of the central trend which defines African literature today in their celebration of human capital as the organising principle of selfhood. Human capital, the idea that

---

[107] Mbembe, *Critique*, p. 71.

[108] The original French uses the same phrase, 'l'autorité de la fiction'. Achille Mbembe, *Critique de la raison nègre* (Paris: La Découverte, 2013), p. 109.

life is no longer mediated or constrained by structural conditions, but rather that 'human beings can themselves transform through skill development, education, creativity, and, perhaps most important of all, *choice*',[109] permeates both texts: from each protagonist's entry into migrancy (in both cases under the auspices of education and, in each case, financed through scholarships – an allegedly meritocratic measure designed to reward and foreground the individual as a self-contained unit), to each's upward mobility, in class, cultural, and social terms, both Ifemelu and Julius are figured as the consummate 'entrepreneur[s] of [their] own human capital, responsible for [their] personal development',[110] unfettered and free. Despite the suffering evinced in the eruption of past memories and ruminations on lost ties to family and community, both characters are developed through their own individualistic productivity in the marketplace of life, a development which the text may implicitly critique (at least in the case of *Open City*), but which nonetheless overdetermines its reading. Of course, an author should not be obliged to write politics into their literary works nor must every African novel be political; however, there is something to be said about the extent to which it is precisely those texts which at least superficially erode and evacuate political context that become celebrated exemplars of the field in the global market. These are, despite the traces of violence beneath their narrative surfaces, novels which flatter liberal notions of the individual as entrepreneur of his or her own life, the idea of human capital and of meritocracy, of choice and of the marketplace of ideas. These are novels which submerge the political in favour of the cultural and the psychological, furthering the perceived chasm between these areas and

---

[109] Lester K. Spence, *Knocking the Hustle: Against the Neoliberal Turn in Black Politics* (New York: Punctum Books, 2016), p. 9.

[110] Spence, p. 113.

minimising their very interconnections and entanglements.[111] These texts demonstrate the ways in which the African novel, in the contemporary era, has become that which celebrates fluidity, celebrates human capital, and which, against the will to ignorance about the continent, erases the possibility for a larger reckoning with the ongoing asymmetries and structures of violence which contribute to its exploitation and despoliation which I outlined earlier in this section.

Sociologists of literature since Bourdieu have emphasised the extent to which, in the literary field, the two modes of capital – cultural/symbolic and economic/material – remain not only distinct but more strongly at odds with one another. Works which accrue significant cultural capital, that is, tend to stand in opposition to works where economic capital is inhered (think here of the distinction made between 'literary' and 'mass market' fiction, or between writers such as John Franzen and Dan Brown). Yet, in the making of African literature, these two modes of capital appear to curiously coincide in a mutually reinforcing system in which one mode of capital – the economic – itself functions as a mechanism through which another form – the cultural – is inhered. It is precisely this intertwining of the cultural and economic modes of capital that enables the consecration of monopoly rents on a certain small subset of the wider body of literary production from the continent,[112] championing

---

[111] Another, more recent, example comes in Imbolo Mbue's *Behold the Dreamers* (London: Fourth Estate, 2016). Despite the novel's ostensible novelty in depicting African migrant characters in America whose ultimate unravelling occurs because of their inclusion – rather than exclusion – from the global capitalist economy, the novel nonetheless forges a deliberately apolitical narrative voice which functions through the repetition of clichés of African patriarchal violence and American decadent misery.

[112] David Harvey, *Rebel Cities: From the Right to the City to the Urban Revolution* (London: Verso, 2012), p. 99.

(as I will discuss further in Section 3) the one as worldly, cosmopolitan, and endowed with literary value, and consigning the other to provincialism and localism. Reinforcing this situation is a parallel bifurcation of the role of the African writer, who, as Adesokan argues, is inevitably positioned either as a critic 'of Western representations of African realities', without acknowledging how these very perceptions form 'the cultural basis, in fact, of the very patronage that underwrites the careers of some of these writers', or through what he terms a 'puzzling compulsion to disavow' the very concept of 'African writing'. In both cases, Adesokan identifies a common orientation towards an ideal reader who is 'white, liberal, culturally knowing', and an ostensible disruption of dominant narratives around Africa whose primary 'effect in the long run is to perpetuate that power'.[113] The making of the African literary celebrity after the neoliberal turn is but one example of the ways in which flows of capital coalesce to create enclaves imbued with an outsized proportion of value in a complex global literary field. In Section 3, I will turn my attention to alternatives to this mode of mapping and their implications for the making of the world therein.

3 Alternative Landscapes

Part of what I have been trying to convey in this study thus far is the extent to which African literature, as a subset of the literary field as we know it today, cannot be studied in isolation; rather, African literature must be positioned against a framework of (ir)rationality and (negative) reason defining Africa in a global context, a framework significantly shaped, over the last four centuries,

---

[113] Akin Adesokan, '"I'm Not An African Writer, Damn You!"', *Chronic Books Supplement*, December 2013, www.chimurengachronic.co.za/im-not-an-african-writer-damn-you/, accessed 29 January 2018.

by the continent's position within a larger world system predicated on the proliferation of the global market under capitalism. At the same time, this positioning of African literature must be recalled as simply one story, albeit one with a particular monopoly on visibility in the global North. In my reading, this framework repeats itself in the positioning – or lack thereof – of African literature and literary production within a world literary landscape.[114] Sara Marzagora notes how, 'From the 1990s onwards, critics based in Europe and America increasingly embraced a postmodern conception of identity as socially constructed, and as a consequence grew dissatisfied with a study of literature based on national canons, preferring more fluid and mobile theoretical paradigms',[115] a comment which gestures both towards the erosion of the nation-state under liquid modernity and coheres with Jameson's claim that postmodernity serves as the aesthetic expression of late capitalism.[116] Equally, Marzagora's arguments foreground the rise of individualistic, culturalist modes of understanding that which had previously been examined as structural, political, and economic phenomenon, expressed through a diffuse model for

[114] For more on world literature, see Pheng Cheah, *What is a World? On Postcolonial Literature as World Literature* (Durham: Duke University Press, 2016); Pascale Casanova, *The World Republic of Letters*, translated by Malcolm Debevoise (Cambridge: Harvard University Press, 2007); Beecroft; Emily Apter, *Against World Literature: On the Politics of Untranslatability* (London: Verso, 2013); David Damrosch, *How to Read World Literature* (Oxford: Wiley & Blackwell, 2009); Warwick Research Collective (WReC), *Combined and Uneven Development: Towards a New Theory of World-Literature* (Liverpool: University of Liverpool Press, 2015).

[115] Sara Marzagora, 'African-Language Literatures and the "Transnational Turn" in Euro-American humanities', *Journal of African Cultural Studies*, 27.1 (2015), 40–55 (pp. 40–1).

[116] Bauman, p. 12; Fredric Jameson, *Postmodernism, or, the Cultural Logic of Late Capitalism* (Durham: Duke University Press, 1991), p. 3.

critical practice based on free-flowing modes of connectivity, linguistic ambiva-lence, and play, which seeks both to complicate essentialisms and decentre the locus of solidarity. Marzagora continues:

> African critics too moved from an essentialist conception of identity and nationhood towards social constructionism, but without completely embracing the latter. Identity and nation-hood come with a very heavy ideological baggage in African studies, tied as they are with the history of anti-colonial libera-tion struggles and the fight to reverse colonial displacement. In African studies, therefore, the more extreme forms of decon-struction have been vehemently rejected on political grounds, privileging positions of 'strategic essentialism' instead.[117]

In these comments, Marzagora identifies the tension between the notion of the world as a superseding structure or field for organising cultural and social life to the detriment of economic and political hierarchies and inequalities, and that of internationalism, the recognition of the still-relevant role of the nation-state and national politics (albeit an eroded nation-state), in the bequest of rights and protections to those within its boundaries. When extended to the field of the literary, then, this is a move which creates a binary opposition – or Manichean dualism – between those literatures which are seen as '"narrow" and "periph-eral"' and those seen as '"global" and "connected"'.[118] Marzagora takes the case of Afrophone literature to make her argument, pointing to an important lacuna in scholarship and criticism around African literary production which results in the denigration of those works as provincial; wed to bounded – and therefore less relevant in our global, connected world – interests; and less sophisticated

---

[117] Marzagora, p. 41. [118] Marzagora, p. 41.

than their globe-trotting Europhone contemporaries. I agree fully with this assessment, but would go further to suggest that the question of 'local' versus 'global', as brute, discrete categories, has affected a similar mode of hierarchisation in the consecration of African literature versus literary production, based largely on the politics of location, dissemination, and reception.[119] Here, it is worth recalling with Doreen Massey that local and global are themselves coconstitutive and interweaving categories.[120] When deployed in the binaristic form recounted here earlier, these terms signal less immutable geographic differences than the uneven distribution of the capital which accrues to certain texts, positioned within or outside of the global literary field and their relative engagement with a range of institutions in the formation of taste.[121] When one brings to bear the fact that world literature in its current formulation, in contrast to Goethe's original understanding of the term, appears not to encapsulate the so-called established or central literatures of North America and Western Europe, moreover, encompassing instead the peripheries and semi-peripheries of the global South and former Eastern bloc, its use becomes even more difficult to elucidate, suggesting that the national and regional literatures of *these* places are less than or lesser, and that *these* places must

---

[119] It is worth noting that I, too, have fallen into this trap. See particularly the chapter entitled 'Global African Literature: Strategies of Address and Cultural Constraints' in Madhu Krishnan, *Contemporary African Literature in English: Global Locations, Postcolonial Identifications* (Basingstoke: Palgrave Macmillan), pp. 130–63.

[120] Doreen Massey, *Space, Place and Gender* (Cambridge: Polity Press, 1994), pp. 146–56.

[121] See, for instance, Nana Wilson-Tagoe, 'Literary Prizes and the Creation of Literary Culture: Judging African Literature in Pan-Commonwealth and Pan-African competitions', *Wasafiri*, 20.46 (2005), 58–61; Doseline Kiguru, 'Literary Prizes, Writers' Organisations and Canon Formation in Africa', *African Studies*, 75.2 (2016) 202–14; Doseline Kiguru, 'Prizing African Literature: Creating a Literary Taste', *Social Dynamics*, 42.1 (2016), 161–74.

somehow come into the world and become worldly. Recalling my discussion of Beecroft in Section 1, then, rather than view the *location* of a text, its content, its implied readership, and its modes of distribution as a cultural issue – as proponents of world literature might encourage us to do – in this section I examine these questions as fundamentally sociopolitical, with significant consequences for the constitution of the literary as a category, aesthetic taste, and the structures of power through which the world is worlded.

As a category, African literature sits uneasily between the national and global scales against which world literature plays, regional in essence, but not in any particularly generative or productive way. Predominant here is the tendency to classify African literature through the lens of postcolonial literature, that which has been described as 'a national literature for a lost empire'.[122] On the one hand, the African case demonstrates the extent to which this may well be true, with a focus on those texts which flatter and soothe postimperial sensibility rather than those which challenge it. On the other hand, however, it is difficult to imagine writing by authors such as Achebe, Ngũgĩ, Soyinka, Aidoo, or their contemporaries as so easily slotted into this imperial nostalgic frame. Perhaps more acute, then, is the tension between what Beecroft identifies as the global and national literary ecologies which emerge with African literature. If, on the one hand, African literature as a quasi-national regional literature seeks to 'create a narrative for a national literature in English out of the colonial experience',[123] itself dependent on a 'universalizing system of notionally discrete identities',[124] it simultaneously functions through a 'forgetting of [its] national origins',[125] fostered through a dominant reading practice which minimises its political import. By this, I mean that, on the one hand, African literature has emerged in part through its singularity or its difference: its authenticity as a representation of a universalised African life,

---

[122] Beecroft, p. 241. [123] Beecroft, p. 199. [124] Beecroft, p. 202. [125] Beecroft, p. 198.

recognisable to global leaders and flattering towards their dispositions. At the same time, however, and particularly recalling the observation that canons are formed by 'identifying entire categories of literature that can be ignored and by establishing criteria for evaluating what remains',[126] African literature has only emerged through the specific evacuation of context, politics, and structures of violence, struggle, and inequity – those very characteristics which mark out the African state and its violent origins.[127]

In an essay published in August 2017 in the open-access online journal *Blindfield*, 'On the African Literary Hustle', Canadian theorist Sarah Brouillette identifies a phenomenon which, inspired by Doreen Strauh's conception of the 'African literary NGO [nongovernmental organisation]',[128] she terms the 'NGOization of African literature'. For Brouillette:

> the recent renaissance in African literature has had little do with development of viable literary readerships in Africa, and viably capitalized production facilities. The post-independence quest to develop literary readerships and publishing and printing trades faced massive hurdles; it was nearly stopped by IMF & World Bank structural adjustment and trade liberalization in the 1990s, and has now been all but abandoned. The field of contemporary Anglophone African literature relies instead on

---

[126] Beecroft, p. 239.

[127] I would argue that this is even the case with those works steeped in the aesthetics of so-called poverty porn, where rather than determine an engagement with the social and political structures underlying these texts, dominant reading practices foreground an affective response predicated on individual feelings of pity.

[128] Doreen Stauhs, *African Literary NGOs: Power, Politics and Participation* (Basingstoke: Palgrave Macmillan, 2013).

private donors, mainly but not exclusively American, support-
ing a transnational coterie of editors, writers, prize judges, event
organizers, and workshop instructors. The literary works that
arise from this milieu of course tend to be targeted at British and
American markets.[129]

The title of Brouillette's essay is a play on 'The African Literary Hustle', issue
43 of the *New Orleans Review*, an issue dedicated to showcasing the 'kaleido-
scopic range of activities' which are too often effaced by the institutional
structures of mediation which determine the extroverted vision of African
literature as a global market category. Editors Laura Murphy and Mũkoma
wa Ngũgĩ explain their intention, in devising the issue, 'to provoke some
interesting and unpredictable writing and thinking that would reflect and
respond to the spirit of the hustle', providing an outlet for authors who 'have
moved on from those stale modes that defined the supposed canon of African
literature' and 'left African literary criticism behind' in favour of writing which
speaks from 'their own times and pleasures', their lived realities.[130] And yet, for
a critic like Brouillette, this very notion of a disinterested or detached 'time and
pleasure' outside of an asymmetrically-loaded world system can be little more
than a pipe dream, always-already mediated by the material realities which
impede the construction of an autonomous African publishing industry. What
results is a mode of aesthetic address invariably targeted at the Euro-American
(or Anglo-American) consumer and the erosion of the possibility of a viable/

---

[129] Sarah Brouillette, 'On the African Literary Hustle', *Blindfield Journal*, 14 August
2017, www.blindfieldjournal.com/2017/08/14/on-the-african-literary-hustle/,
accessed 31 January 2018.

[130] Mũkoma wa Ngũgĩ and Laura T. Murphy, 'Introducing Issue 43: This Hustle Is Not
Your Grandpa's African Lit', *New Orleans Review*, 43 (2017), www.neworleansre
view.org/this-hustle-is-not-your-grandpas-african-lit/, accessed 29 January 2018.

visible market elsewhere. Put slightly differently, because Anglophone African literature 'relies on private donors' (here, Brouillette is referring to the Ford Foundation's prior – and now defunct – funding of Kenya's Kwani Trust, founded by Binyavanga Wainaina, which I discuss below), and because many of its key figures inhabit some mode of mobility in their lived experiences, it must, 'of course' be 'targeted at British and American markets'. While these are important arguments, particularly in the ways in which they gesture towards the neoliberal structures which determine the contours of the literary hustle, which I will discuss below, there is equally a danger that this economically deterministic vision of literary production functions to the detriment of the networks of entanglement which remain oriented towards and located on the African continent, reinforcing their lack of visibility to popular and critical discourse rooted in the global North.

In this section, then, I aim to extend these arguments by provoking thinking about whether it is possible to engage in a critical analysis of African literature in an institutional landscape which is *not* mediated by a centre/periphery topography as its default position and to think about the canon of African literature beyond the North/South binary. What would an African literature based around, against, and towards African institutions – and the institution of African literature therein – look like?[131] What forms – aesthetic and material – might emerge? What possibilities could inhere in a view of the African literary landscape in which the primary interlocutors for literary production and primary drivers of valuation function against a different kind

---

[131] Here, I draw on the distinction made between the noun and verb form of institution in Peter D. McDonald, 'Instituting (World) Literature', in *Institutions of World Literature: Writing, Translation, Markets*, ed. by Stefan Helgesson and Pieter Vermeulen (London: Routledge, 2015), pp. 39–52 (pp. 39–42).

of topography? How might this impact upon the ways in which we think about literary canons and canon formation?

Since 2016 I have been involved in several collaborative projects with a broad range of literary producers and activists based on the African continent, primarily in Uganda, South Africa, Kenya, Cameroon, and Côte d'Ivoire. The remainder of this section draws heavily on these experiences and the insights which I have derived from this work, which comprise a series of interrelated, collaborative projects which specifically seek to bring scholars and practitioners in dialogue. While my own practice as a literary scholar has not previously delved into the implications of this kind of participatory and observational practice, my argument in what follows is that the discursive and material forms of position-taking, networks of engagement, and citational-critical matrices which these projects have enabled me to access provide crucial information for a fuller and more robust understanding of the politics of canonisation and consecration which I have been discussing in this study. As a scholar based in the global North, whose primary academic interlocutors share this location, I contend in what remains of this section that integrating material gathered through personal conversations, workshops, roundtables, and fieldwork in this manner is essential to the task of raising visibility around the diversity of work performed by literary producers and activists based on the continent and, by so doing, complicating what is too often still a simplistic picture of African literature (and the very notion of knowledge production), writ large.

The conversations which have emerged from these projects suggest that it is indeed possible to identify models, structures, networks, and fields of African literary production which do not easily or exactly conform to the strictures of the global literary marketplace or the precepts of the global literary field. What these observations indicate, instead, is that the literary field, while radically asymmetrical in the patterns under which capital of all kinds is distributed therein, is not all-subsuming nor all-powerful and that multiple spaces remain for the forging of alternative – or lateral – networks, fields, topographies, and publics to function beyond a single frame of relationality and valuation. Actors and agents engaged in literary production, moreover, are not entirely passive, at the mercy of the marketplace and the puissance of the global North or centres of the world republic of letters, but are able to act in ways which are novel, agonistic, and often far more complex than extant discussions of the literary allow space to fully comprehend. Recalling Cooper's point that 'asymmetry is not dichotomy',[132] rather than view literary production as occurring through an inevitable assimilation of norms which emanate from the historical centres of power and capital, the remainder of this section is driven by the attempt to conceptualise a different way of thinking about the literary, as a category, such that the activities undertaken by continentally-based producers and consumers can be rendered legible within the larger field. This task, in turn, centres on an attempt to think of African literary production and the literary field not as being dominated by a disinterested notion of world literature but by a more complex and multiaxial concept of literary internationalism and internationalist solidarity, with a rooting in the range of claims to world formation which have operated on the African continent across history.[133]

In my own research, three areas emerge which bear significantly on the ways in which we might think about the place of African literary production in a global literary market: the question of funding and its impact upon the means

---

[132] Frederick Cooper, 'Africa's Pasts and Africa's Historians', *Canadian Journal of African Studies / Revue Canadienne des Études Africaines*, 34.2 (2000), 298–336 (p. 300).

[133] See, for instance, Ferguson; Frederick Cooper, *Decolonization and African Society: The Labor Question in French and British Africa* (Cambridge: Cambridge University Press, 1996).

of literary production and dissemination; the forging of an aesthetic vision which attempts to open the notion of the literary to new possibilities and definitions; and the role of networks of influence, collaboration, and creativity. Here, I begin by tracing some of the contours of these arguments before considering a few examples of literary collectives and initiatives based on the African continent which exemplify the complex means through which these issues are navigated. This not, of course, to suggest an entirely optimistic vision of literary production on the African continent after the neoliberal turn. Significant barriers remain and the distribution of capital, in a global context, remains radically asymmetrical in its manifestations. As Emma Shercliff, drawing on her work with Nigerian publishers, notes, 'three issues surfaced repeatedly [in discussions of the major barriers faced by continental institutions]: the cost of doing business in Nigeria (high price of paper, high price of ink, tariffs & import duties); the failure of government to understand what publishers do (as exemplified by the recent book import tax debacle, little distinction is made between the role of the publisher and that of the printer) and difficulties with the distribution of books (poor transport systems, weak bookselling networks, lack of decent bookstores)'.[134] At the same time, my work with literary producers has suggested that those of us based in the institutions of the global North often approach this context from a perspective rooted in a priori conceptions of norms and structures, which serves to occlude the visibility and larger dynamism of the picture on the ground. Shercliff's own work, notably the digital publishing of the *Valentine's Day Anthology* by Ankara Press, attests to the variety of means and strategies deployed by producers on the

---

[134] Emma Shercliff, 'The Valentine's Day Anthology: A Snapshot of the Possibilities and Challenges of African Publishing', *Africa in Words*, 5 March 2015, www.africainwords.com/2015/03/05/the-valentines-day-anthology-a-snapshot-of-the-possibilities-and-challenges-of-african-publishing/, accessed 29 January 2018.

continent, citing the ways in which nontraditional and digital modes of publishing 'allow [...] a publisher a freedom that would be impossible for the more traditional, large educational publishers' through its speed to market, collaborative format, potential for distribution, and the possibilities for innovation in content and language that it brings.[135] In Section 2 of this study, my discussions of the potential for digital space to democratise African literature and literary production remained sceptical, particularly with respect to the impact of digital technology on the gatekeeping practices which mediate its emergence. It is nonetheless the case, following Shercliff's recollections of her own experience as a publisher on the African continent, that the potential for innovation – particularly in language, genre, and distribution – should not be outright discounted.[136]

A primary driver of the tendency to view literary production through the lens of a centre/periphery spatial ecology emanates from the lack of sustainable, continentally based funding streams for producers, activists, and creatives. Brouillette, for instance, argues that even ostensibly independent initiatives like Kenya's Kwani Trust and other literary NGOs function via the same market patterns which have marked the world literary field:

> The situation is one of donor-supported funding of networks of writers who are more dependent on each other as cultural brokers, on international donors, and on foreign markets, than they are on the existence of a local readership for literary works. Kwani Trust print publications are sold in bookshops,

---

[135] Shercliff, 'The Valentine's Day Anthology'.

[136] Zahrah Nesbitt-Ahmed, 'Reclaiming African Literature in the Digital Age: An Exploration of Online Literary Platforms', *Critical African Studies*, 9.3 (2017), 377–90.

convenience stores, and supermarkets in Nairobi, and in select shops in Mombasa, but Kenya's rural population is 77.8%. They are also sold online, but only 9 out of 100 people in Kenya have internet access. [23] The current issue of *Kwani?* is $17 USD, and a recent Kwaninis title – this is a spinoff pocketsize series – is $10 USD, which is too steep for the majority of Kenyans, where, the UN reports, the average daily earnings work out to about $4 USD, and most people live below the poverty line. As Strauhs points out – and at the risk stating the obvious – the people involved in the Trust's advancement possess 'habitus, economic situation, and social status' that are 'dramatically different from the majority of the Kenyan population'.[137]

Founded in 2003, Kwani Trust developed out of a series of debates by writers, journalists, teachers, activists, and literary enthusiasts who together 'pondered the state of Kenya's literary scene'.[138] Lasting over a period of years, these discussions coalesced when, following his award of the 2002 Caine Prize for African Writing (a UK-based prize founded in memory of former Booker plc Chairman Michael Caine, which seeks 'to bring African writing to a wider audience' through an annual £10,000 short story award),[139] Kwani founder Binyavanga Wainaina secured funding from the Ford Foundation's Special Initiatives for Africa programme, which has subsequently come to an end. This, in turn, led to the establishment of the Trust and publication of the flagship

---

[137] Brouillette, 'On the African Literary Hustle'.

[138] Kwani Trust, 'Our History', www.kwani.org/our-history/kwani.htm, accessed 29 January 2018.

[139] The Caine Prize For African Writing, 'About Us', www.caineprize.com/about/, accessed 29 January 2018.

Kwani? journal, first online and then very quickly moving to print. Kate Haines Wallis has extensively chronicled the entangled networks of capital, influence, and intimacy which led to Kwani Trust's emergence as a key driver of independent literary production in East Africa,[140] and I will not recount this detailed and meticulous research here. Rather, my interest is to consider the seemingly intractable opposition between Kwani Trust's own mission to open new spaces for literary activity on the continent and Brouillette's assertions, above.

That Kwani Trust's official establishment relied upon an influx of international donor money is no outlier in the realm of African literary production; multinational donor organisations, including the Goethe Foundation and Miles Moreland Foundation, remain important avenues of funding for African cultural producers across the continent. Central to Brouillette's critique is a sense in which the directionality of funding must in some way impact upon the directionality of address and aesthetic formations. On a certain level, it is difficult to argue with this assertion, and certainly the statistics and figures recounted above paint a grim picture. Yet, the lack of sustainable funding outlets for literary and creative production is hardly unique to the African continent, something that Brouillette's own published research makes plain.[141] Equally, an understanding of the self-reported positionality and directionality of literary producers themselves enables a better understanding of what may be a more complex dynamic at play. In the case of Kwani Trust,

---

[140] Kate Wallis, 'How Books Matter: Kwani Trust, Farafina, Cassava Republic and the Medium of Print', *Wasafiri*, 31.4 (2016), 39–46; Kate Wallis, 'Exchanges in Nairobi and Lagos'.

[141] See, for instance, Sarah Brouillette, 'Neoliberalism and the Demise of the Literary', in *Neoliberalism and Contemporary Literary Culture*, ed. by Mitchum Huehls and Rachel Greenwald Smith (Baltimore: Johns Hopkins University Press, 2017), pp. 277–90.

for instance, it is notable that distribution networks remain deliberately centred on Kenya and a select group of continentally based partners, including South Africa's *Chimurenga* and Nigeria's Cassava Republic Press.[142] Since *Kwani* 5, a special double issue of the journal dedicated to responding to the 2007 Kenyan presidential elections and its violent aftermath, moreover, each issue of the journal has focused on a single theme with particular resonance in the nation.[143] On one level, systems of patronage have long driven literary production in a range of geographies and historical periods; in this sense, the idea that African writers and producers might be reliant on donor funding is nothing new and suggests instead a longer continuity with the historical landscape of funding and economic support which has mediated literary writing. Equally, it is possible to view the directionality of funding not as a problem but as part of a longer process of the redistribution of capital, part of the range of restitutions to which the African continent is owed. In April 2017, for instance, I convened a workshop in Cape Town as part of the Arts and Humanities Research Council (AHRC) Research Network 'Small Magazines, Literary Networks and Self-Fashioning in Africa and Its Diasporas', which sought to bring together academics and practitioners to examine alternative print histories and their implications for knowledge production and the making of public life on the African continent. During a session on prizes, prestige, and the production of capital, one literary producer argued forcefully that African cultural producers have the responsibility to appropriate funding from the global North as part of their service to the larger project of decolonisation, citing the centuries-long despoliation of the continent as having incurred

---

[142] Kwani Trust, 'Bookstores', www.kwani.org/publications/book-store.htm, accessed 29 January 2018.

[143] *Kwani?* 6 is themed on Kenyan and African writers born after September 1978; *Kwani?* 7 on diasporic imaginaries; and *Kwani?* 8 on the 2013 Kenyan elections

a global debt towards it.[144] Under this reading, to accept funding from a Ford Foundation, Goethe Institute, or Miles Moreland Foundation is less a capitulation to the hegemonic norms of an asymmetrically-loaded system of capital and valuation and more a radical act of reparation and resistance. While recognising that, as another participant at that same event noted, the influx of funding and capital necessarily shifts organisational priorities, formalising what previously functioned more as informal social contracts between like-minded individuals with a collective commitment and thereby running the risk of ossification of practice, it is nonetheless possible to consider a more complex spatiotemporal frame through which to view the flows of capital and investments.

My conversations with literary producers, particularly those of the younger generation, suggest that much – if not most – literary activity on the continent remains viewed by its purveyors primarily as taking the shape of passion projects driven by political commitment, rather than a desire to generate revenue. Time and again, literary entrepreneurs and activists note that their own initiatives only survive because of the time, capital, and effort they are willing to bring to their projects, motivated by a wish to open up the space for new stories, new debates, and new modes of citationality to proliferate. Emmanual Iduma, one of the founders of the Nigeria-based *Saraba* magazine, for instance, notes that the driving aim behind the project came from both the desire to 'do something for Nigeria' and the realisation that many young and unpublished writers were producing work 'with a kind of context that American literary journals or British literary journals did not want'. In response to this situation, *Saraba* was born as a platform 'to publish writing that only a Nigerian or an African magazine could find

---

[144] Bond, pp. 55–6.

interest in', growing out of and supported by its founders' personal funds.[145] Similarly, the editors of *The Single Story Foundation Journal* note the importance of offering 'opportunities to accommodate the exploding literary culture that is sweeping the African landscape and diaspora', detailing their effort to 'open a literary dialogue' through a complex process of workshopping and mentorship.[146] The organisers of the Ba re e ne re Literature Festival in Lesotho, meanwhile, self-describe their efforts as a hustle driven by patience, hard work, and a commitment to the creation of spaces 'where connections are forged and conversations carry out into the streets'.[147] For many of my interlocutors, this recourse to self-funding forms an important element of the effort to operate outside of extant institutional structures and, as *Chimurenga* founder Ntone Edjabe highlights, 'to create and develop alternative distribution networks with others like ourselves', possibilities which might be foreclosed if the outfit were reliant on extant structures and institutions.[148] *Chimurenga* subsequently was awarded the 2011 Prince Claus Fund Prize in recognition of these efforts.

At the forefront of these concerns is the question of sustainability in the face of reliance on donor funding on the one hand, and the need for financial

---

[145] Kate Haines, 'Q&A: Emmanuel Iduma – Writer and Co-Founder of *Saraba Magazine*', *Africa in Words*, 15 October 2015, www.africainwords.com/2013/10/15/qa-emmanuel-iduma-writer-and-co-founder-of-saraba-magazine/, accessed 29 January 2018.

[146] Tiah Marie Beautement, 'Editor's Note', *Tssf Journal*, 1 (2017), 3–4 (p. 3).

[147] Lineo Segoete, 'Ba re e ne re: Building a Community of Writers and Readers in Lesotho', *Africa in Words*, 23 May 2017, www.africainwords.com/2017/05/22/ba-re-e-ne-re-building-a-community-of-writers-and-readers-in-lesotho/, accessed 29 January 2018.

[148] Robert Fraser, '"Who No Know Go Know": An Interview with Ntone Edjabe', *Wasafiri*, 22.3 (2007), 62–7 (p. 67).

control in order to maintain full artistic autonomy on the other.[149] A wealth of inventive responses have arisen in response, ranging from the rise of self-publishing outlets; to the leveraging of social media and personal appearances in the name of marketing and publicity; to the use of reciprocal networks and agreements across collectives and publications. Critical accounts of these innovations tend to bifurcate along two lines, either following the self-reported positioning of practitioners themselves, viewing them as a means of rejecting the precepts of the global literary market in the formation of African literature, avoiding its attempts to project and define African writing and innovating the ways in which books are distributed and sold,[150] on the one hand, or, on the other, as a capitulation to the neoliberal implications of the aforementioned literary hustle, with its imperative to displace structural inequities onto the figure of the individualist entrepreneur. For Spence, for instance, the notion of the hustle is characteristic of a more profound transformation in how labour – black labour specifically – has been conceptualised after the neoliberal turn. Labour, under this definition, is a constant process, an imperative for the individual responsible for their own success and a mentality which those 'with no role in the formal economy need to possess in order to survive and thrive'.[151] Under this reading, the hustle is another element in a larger economy which erases the institutional forces which contribute to structural inequality in

---

[149] In August 2017 at the second annual Arts Management and Literary Activism (AMLA) workshop, run by the Kampala-based Center for African Cultural Excellence and of which I served as a facilitator along with Bwesigye bwa Mwesigire and Kate Haines Wallis, one of the guest facilitators repeatedly stressed this point, arguing that without financial autonomy, creative control could only ever be partial.

[150] Zachary Rosen, 'Abdi Latif Ega and the Rejection of the "African" Novel', *Africa is a Country*, 24 February 2016, www.africasacountry.com/2016/02/abdi-latif-ega-and-the-rejection-of-the-african-novel/, accessed 29 January 2018.

[151] Spence, p. 2.

favour of a vision of the individual as entrepreneur of the self. With this reading in mind, however, it appears that the African literary producer enters a no-win situation, unable to escape the forces of the neoliberal turn, whether in the receipt of donor funding or in a capitulation to the marketisation of selfhood though the hustle. Yet, there is another way in which to view these attempts on the part of literary producers to forge new ways of working and new forms of collaboration, one intertwined with the longer historical import of shadow economies, shadow spaces, and shadow networks, which function as a redress to official and institutional exclusions on the African continent.[152]

A key element which develops across the diverse body of activities which comprise African literary production is a focus on forging new corridors of collaboration and coproduction of knowledge, functioning ultimately as the basis for a new mode of internationalist, pan-Africanist solidarity. Cape Town-based Chimurenga, a self-described 'project-based mutable object, a print magazine, a workspace, and platform for editorial and curatorial activities', for instance, can be defined by what has been called its 'unapologetically pan-African' ethos,[153] one based on the effort to follow in the footsteps of earlier outfits including *Transition* and *Black Orpheus* in the task of 'imagin[ing] a world as much as [...] report[ing] it'.[154] With its name taken from the

---

[152] Ato Quayson, *Oxford Street, Accra: City Life and the Itineraries of Transnationalism* (Durham: Duke University Press, 2014), p. 201; Basile Ndjio, 'Carrefour de la joie: Popular Deconstruction of the African Postcolonial Public Sphere', *Africa: Journal of the International African Institute*, 74.3 (2005), 265–94.

[153] Dzekashu MacViban, 'Q & A with Ntone Edjabe on *Chimurenga*, Fela, and Politics', *Bakwa Magazine*, 18 August 2012, www.bakwamagazine.com/2012/08/18/conver sation-ntone-edjabe-by-breaking-the-divide-between-the-public-and-the-private-he-fela-expanded-our-vocabulary-of-resistance-the-musician-was-no-longer-sim ply-an-entertainer/, accessed 29 January 2018.

[154] MacViban.

Shona word for freedom struggle and its tagline, 'Who No Know No Go' from the music and lyrics of Nigerian Afrobeat pioneer Fela Kuti, *Chimurenga*'s very foundation marks this striving. Based upon the forging of a transcontinental network of friends, conspirators, and collaborators, *Chimurenga*, in the words of its founder (himself a Nigerian-educated Cameroonian resident in South Africa), strives to 'mainstream [their] own aesthetics and reduce [their] dependency on the global publishing system',[155] leveraging partnerships with Kwani Trust, Cassava Republic Press, and numerous others both on and outside of the continent to circumvent the systems of distribution which silo and divide Africa's many geographies. As Edjabe notes:

> These are friends and like-minded publishing projects – by developing editorial projects together and assisting each other in areas such as distribution, we quietly mainstream our own aesthetics and reduce our dependency on the global publishing system. At present it is difficult for a Nigerian author to be read in Kenya unless they're published by a London or New York based mega-house. I think it's also important to revive the spirit of solidarity that was alive during the 1960s and 70s – and regain the capacity to imagine and shape our own futures.[156]

Chimurenga editor Stacy Hardy's recollection of her path to involvement with the collective is telling in this regard. Characterising herself as a relatively new and unhappy resident in Cape Town, Hardy describes her first encounter with Chimurenga at Clarke's Bookshop on Long Street as her entryway into an alternative community, based not on easy political or geographical affiliations, but on a different, revolutionary pan-Africanist ideal. *Chimurenga*'s vitality, for

---

[155] MacViban. [156] Macviban.

Hardy, comes from the free-flowing nature of its intellectualism and its relative freedom as an outfit based outside of the academy and traditional publication structures, allowing new thinking to emerge and novel, innovative generic juxtapositions to emerge which promote the production of knowledge beyond the disciplinary distinctions across journalism, theory, and fiction.[157] With the Chimurenga library, an alternative archive of pan-African independent print culture which functions as 'an ongoing invention into knowledge production and the archive that seeks to re-imagine the library as a laboratory for extended curiosity, new adventures, critical thinking, daydreaming, sociopolitical involvement, partying and random perusal' and today includes a number of extended research projects on the creation of public culture on the continent;[158] the *African Cities Reader*, 'a biennial publication that brings together contributors from across Africa and the world to challenge the prevailing depiction of urban life on the continent and redefine cityness, Africa-style';[159] the Pan African Space Station, 'a periodic, pop-up live radio studio; a performance and exhibition space; a research platform and living archive, as well as an ongoing, internet based radio station';[160] and its quarterly broadsheet, *The Chronic*, which I will discuss below,

---

[157] Comments made as part of the 'Personal Histories, Personal Archives, Alternative Print Cultures' roundtable held at the Chimurenga offices in Cape Town on 3 April 2017. The conversation was broadcast and recorded for Chimurenga's Pan-African Space Station and is summarised here: Sara Smit, 'Finding Affiliations: Reading Communities, Literary Institutions & Small Magazines', *Africa in Words*, 21 October 2017, www.africainwords.com/2017/10/21/finding-affiliations-reading-communities-literary-institutions-small-magazines/, accessed 29 January 2018.

[158] Chimurenga Library, 'About', www.chimurengalibrary.co.za/about, accessed 29 January 2018.

[159] *African Cities Reader*, www.africancitiesreader.org.za/, accessed 29 January 2018.

[160] Pan African Space Station, www.panafricanspacestation.org.za/, accessed 29 January 2018.

Chimurenga marks one mode of world-creation which both expands the notion of the literary and cultivates networks of friendship and intimacy towards a new way of experiencing and thinking the world.

To date, *Chimurenga* and its associated projects have developed pan-African partnerships which expand its remit to the Francophone, Germanophone, and Arabic worlds, promoting the reawakening of historical solidarities actively discouraged under colonialism and tacitly broken down by the structures of mainstream publishing initiatives. This form of remapping, a reworlding of the world, is central to the work of African literary production. In Cameroon, for instance, *Bakwa* Magazine, which has today expanded to the Bakwacast, a seasonal podcast, and Bakwa Books, has engaged in collaborative partnerships with Mexico-based online magazine *Ofi*, California-based Phoenome Media, and Nigeria-based *Saraba* magazine, with whom they launched the Literary Exchange Project, an effort to foster dialogue and exchange between a younger generation of Nigerian and Cameroonian writers as a mode of restitution against the colonialist manoeuvres which historically divided the two contiguous nation-states. It is no coincidence that across conversations with literary producers, notions of friendship and intimacy appear as recurrent trends, enabling a continual process of creation, emergence, and transformation. The Jalada collective, for instance, whose most recent publications include the 'Fear Issue', published in collaboration with *Transtition* magazine (currently housed at Harvard University), was born out of a meeting of young writers from Kenya, Uganda, Zimbabwe, South Africa, and Nigeria at a workshop held in Nairobi and convened by Kwani Trust, Granta, and the British Council. In West Africa, former editors at Farafina Trust, which ran the short-lived eponymous magazine, have founded such new publishing ventures as Narrative Landscape Press and Parrésia Publishers.[161] Across these activities and institutions,

---

[161] Nathan Suhr-Sytsma, '"A Secret History of the Nation": Small Magazines at Writivism 2017', *Africa in Words*, www.africainwords.com/2017/10/30/a-secret-

what appears is the emergence of a complex network of collaboration, coproduction, and shared ideology, forging topographies which are not so easily defined in terms of the local, the regional, or the global, but which attest instead to the complex streams, flows, and enclaves of capital and exchange which allow literary production to emerge. Following Kate Haines Wallis, it is moreover important to highlight that flows and networks function not merely to displace capital from the global North to South, or vice versa, but to produce a new mode of cartography for the world as perceived by these literary producers.[162]

Each of these initiatives demonstrates the importance of an aesthetic vision and conception of the literary which moves beyond its extant definition. Beecroft has shown that the concept of the literary, despite its commonplace usage, has never been either static or uncontested.[163] In the context of African literary production, the literary functions both as an element on the page, tied to writing, but also as a lived, and living, archive comprised of various modes of production (written, oral, visual) and mediated across multiple modes. Kwani, Bakwa, and Chimurenga, as well as other literary collectives including Praxis Magazine, Saraba, and Writivism, function not merely as publishing outlets, but also as prize-awarding establishments, workshops, mentoring networks, and live literature productions, with literary nights, open mic nights, festivals, and more, which leverage oral, popular, visual, and print forms to produce a notion of the literary as a mediating site through which publics and citational-critical matrices are constituted. Productions such as the Jalada Mobile Festival, for instance, which combined a series of city-based mini-festivals with activities centred around a mobile bus tour, or the Upright People Movement, an initiative inspired

history-of-the-nation-small-magazines-at-writivism-2017/, accessed 29 January 2018.

[162] Wallis, 'Exchanges in Nairobi and Lagos'. [163] Beecroft, pp. 203–5.

by the Ngũgĩ wa Thiong'o short story of the same name (not coincidentally the kernel for the Jalada Translation Project, which saw the story translated into more than thirty indigenous African languages) and which seeks to leverage literary production as a means of reconstituting notions of indigeneity, demand modes of critical inquiry which move beyond orthodox models of textual criticism and literary mapping. These in-person and face-to-face elements offer another way to understand the literary as collaborative and living, alive beyond the page and beyond the boundaries in order to create something new, while simultaneously foregrounding the multiplicity of modes of consecration which continue to mediate its emergence. This mode of newness is evident in the aesthetic principles which guide these initiatives, principles based on the levelling of generic divisions across visual art, interview, journalism, commentary, fiction, and creative nonfiction though the fabrication of online, aural, and print spaces. By making the aesthetic, institution-building, and collaborative work of these collectives and enterprises visible, then, what might begin to emerge is a shift in the ways in which African literature is conceptualised, both in terms of its own contours and its practice of world formation (the formation, that is, of Africa as world). Despite the outsized proportion of symbolic capital which continues to accrue to the institutions of the global North, moreover, this mode of visibility serves as a redress to the tendency to neglect the import of home-grown institutions such as Chimurenga, Saraba, Writivism, Farafina (not to mention Facebook and WhatsApp groups) in enabling the creation of the very material which enables the institutions of the global North, such as the aforementioned Caine Prize, to flourish. It may be tempting to read this as another element in the longer history of material exploitation of the continent as a repository of raw materials for manufacture elsewhere, but I would argue that both the self-positioning of literary activists on the continent and the robust and complex nature of their work suggests a more nuanced picture. In this sense, increasing their visibility is a crucial element of developing a broader and more robust understanding of the literary and literary field.

In what remains of this section, I turn to close readings of Chimurenga across two of its incarnations: the eponymous magazine, which ran from 2002 to 2011, and its current form, *The Chronic*, a quarterly periodical founded in 2013 which takes the form of a broadsheet newspaper and its supplement sections. *Chimurenga* was initially born as a one-off print book, whose success led to the publication of fifteen subsequent issues. Its founder recalls its institution as follows:

> It began with pretty much a collective frustration. I was free-lancing as a journalist at the time, concentrating on cultural affairs, music, literature and so on. But there was very little space in the newspapers here in the late 1990s in which to confront anything whatsoever. The prevalent mood was more one of reconciliation – to forgive and, when possible, to forget. So it became really urgent for me as a writer to create a space for some of this stuff that would never get published in the main-stream media. Not only contemporary work, but also some work that never got published in the first place because of the history we are aware of. I may have taken it on as a personal quest, but I know many other writers and journalists shared this feeling – Sandile Dikeni, Lesego Rampolokeng, Gael Reagon and others who contributed to the first issue. Luckily I was not in a job at the time, so I could just go ahead and set it up.[164]

[164] Fraser, 'Who No Know Go Know', p. 63.

Central to the magazine's work is the idea that it serves as a crucible for the creation of alternative communities of engagement, forging them beyond the nation-state and in a manner not based on easy geographical or political affiliation. At its core, the magazine seeks a form of intellectualism not based on the academy, but on the free movement of thought, giving rise to different modes of juxtaposition and valuation, refusing generic distinctions, and producing new modes of knowledge production by so doing. Generated from a series of personal conversations and friendships, the magazine assembles these intimate moments into a sharable object to be distributed to a wider public who, too, become interpellated into the Chimurenga community. Encapsulated in its first issue, 'Music is the Weapon', which contains essays, short fictional pieces, poetic reflections, and more, which span a wild and often bewildering trajectory of pan-African internationalist affiliations to create a radically open archive of the present, positioned in multiple directions and towards multiple collectives, sometimes oppositional and always radically open. The ethos by which the magazine functions might be summed up in a quotation from the first essay within its pages, a reflection on the South African musical icon Brenda Fassie:

> The obliteration of the divide between the private and the public is at the bottom of her verbal ungovernability. Indeed, if the state is to be rendered ungovernable, and if that ungovernability is a factor not only of the intension to be free, but also that the act of rendering the state ungovernable is itself an act of freedom, then Brenda's voice enters the public arena as ungovernable, the ultimate expression of personal freedom. While she may shock, she is at the same time admired, not for her courage (for this is not courage at

play), but for being representative of the value of expressiveness.[165]

Chimurenga, then, might be interpreted as a form of this very ungovernability. Versus the modes of ordering and relationality implied within the world republic of letters or canon of African literatures, here emerges the idea of a different way of thinking internationalism and radical aesthetics, inspired by the longer histories of pan-African solidarity, but entirely new. Rather than a table of contents, issue one boasts a tracklisting on its back cover, listing contributions ranging from a history of South African jazz, to pieces on Fela Kuti, George Clinton, Peter Tosh, and reggae as a political movement to political commentary on colourism and La Franc-Maçonnerie. Featuring writing in translation (and sometimes untranslated or multilingual), as well as reprints of forgotten essays that once 'circulated [...] originally through informal networks, but [were] never really in a journal or a book',[166] *Chimurenga* functions both as a reconstitution of the archive of pan-African internationalism and as a new point of entry through which to understand the cultural politics of location which mediate the emergence of African literary production. This ethos is repeated across the pages of the magazine over its full run, culminating in issue 15, 'The Curriculum is Everything', which takes the form of a school textbook in order to curate a missing archive of cultural-political engagement that undoes and rescripts the idea of knowledge as a site of rational ordering and market exchange.

The sixteenth issue of *Chimurenga*, titled the 'Chimurenga Chronicle', takes the form of a broadsheet newspaper. Published in 2011, it asks its

---

[165] Njabulo Ndebele, 'Thinking of Brenda', *Chimurenga 1: Music is the Weapon*, (2002), pp. 1–6 (p. 5).

[166] Fraser, 'Who No Know Go Know', p. 63.

contributors to take themselves back to 2008, responding to the wave of xenophobic violence that struck across South Africa that time. The editors describe this issue as a time machine, moving from 2011 to 2008, responding to an increasing sense of urgency around the publication's reach and publics, driven by political and ideological expediencies. In a keynote lecture delivered at the University of Bristol in 2018, Stacy Hardy described how the editors deliberately leveraged local Somali shop networks as stockists of the publication and mobilised a network of street sellers to move beyond the vestiges of traditional modes of distribution and traditional literary audiences.[167] Faced with a need for a literary practice whose speed might be more proportionate to the speed of the world and its transformations, able to intervene into the public domain through the temporality of the contemporary, the newspaper form thus enables the fabrication of different topographies and temporalities, forging a different kind of historical archive and different kind of public sphere. The newspaper, moreover, enables the creation of novel matrices of citationality and critical discourse; a newspaper can be left in a café or bus, discarded for a new reader on a public bench, its sections removeable, and its ordering changed.

On its website, *The Chronic*'s origins story is described in some detail:

> When will the new emerge – and if it is already here, how do we decipher it? In which ways do people live their lives with joy and creativity and beauty, sometimes amid suffering and violence, and sometimes perpendicular to it? How do people

---

[167] Stacy Hardy, 'Stacy Hardy in Conversation with Billy Kahora', keynote lecture at the Small Magazines, Literary Networks and Self-Fashioning in Africa and its Diasporas conference, 20 January 2018, Bristol, United Kingdom.

fashion routines and make sense of the world in the face of the temporariness or volatility that defines so many of the arrangements of social existence here?

These questions loom over a contemporary Africa. Yet most knowledge produced on the continent remains heavily reliant on simplistic and rigid categories unable to capture the complexities that inflect so much of contemporary quotidian life here.[168]

These questions are directly reckoned with in the March 2015 edition of *The Chronic*, 'New Cartographies'. Throughout its pages, the issue imagines a world in which 'maps were made by Africans for their own use, to understand and make visible their own realities or imaginaries'.[169] Accompanied by long-form journalism and creative writing, the maps presented in the issue offer a powerful redress to the historical isolation of the continent as a seeming excess to the world system, whose very contingency is made plain in 'A Brief History of Mapping', the opening essay by Stacy Hardy:

> Sitting in the ruin of the once great library of Alexandria in Egypt, around CE 150, the Greek astronomer Claudius Ptolemaeus wrote a treatise entitled *Geography*: this was a topographical account of the latitude and longitude of more than 8,000 nations in Europe, Asia and Africa; an explanation of the role of astronomy in geography; a detailed mathematical guide to making maps;

---

[168] *Chimurenga Chronic*, 'About', www.chimurengachronic.co.za/about/, accessed 29 January 2018.

[169] *Chimurenga Chronic*, 'The Chronic: New Cartographies March 2015', www.chimurenga.co.za/product/the-chronic-new-cartographies-march-2015, accessed 29 January 2018.

and the treatise that provided the Western geographical tradition with an enduring definition of geography.

> The definition didn't hold up with the American academy. In 1948, Harvard University officials shut down its geography department after being flummoxed by the 'inability to extract a clear definition of the subject, to grasp the substance of geography, or to determine its boundaries with other disciplines'.[170]

In what follows, Hardy underscores the very mutability and ingraspability of cartography, running through a sweeping account of the maps which have produced the world through history: Islamic accounts heavily influenced by Greek and Indo-Persian traditions; the Mercator projection, with the northern hemisphere dominating; the Fuller Dymaxion projection as a redress; Torres-Garcia's Inverted Map of South America, which flips the world on its head; the immutable colonial maps produced by the Berlin Conference of 1884–5 (at which, ironically, no actual maps were made); World Bank-sponsored maps of resource-rich regions; Cyon's Alt-Africa map; and ending with a challenge inspired by Mbembe's call that maps shift their orientation from location to the larger movements of global politics and economics. Featuring a range of alternative maps which explore non-statist armed conflict; the web of Qaddhafi's political and economic influence across the continent; the geography of – and conflict over – water, oil, and other mineral resources; drug ports; soccer cities; new modes of supra- and a-national territoriality; cultural institutions and neoimperial geographies of soft power; and lines of inward migration and repatriation, the issue constitutes precisely such an answer. Taken as a whole, these maps enable a vision of the continent which attends to the global

---

[170] Stacy Hardy, 'A Brief History of Mapping', *The Chronic*, March 2015, p. 2.

flows and enclaves of capital, power, people, and images which together produce the African continent as a contested and inherently heterogeneous site of entanglements, enabling a vision of geography in which Guangzhou, China, might lead directly to Kigali, Rwanda, or the African Union, United States, and European Union might all coexist within Somalia.

What publications such as those that I have described in Section 3 – and the experiences of the individuals, collectives, and institutions which produce them – might enable us to see, then, is a broader and more complex vision of African literature, one which demands that we consider the literary through new forms and reorient our cartographical ordering of the world, and the literary field within, to accommodate new definitions and new positions. The very separation of the world of African writing into African literature, the canonised form, and African literary production, that which we might not always perceive, becomes itself another mystification which covers the more complex dynamics of exchange and influence through which creativity and newness emerge. If critical and popular accounts of African literature are not always capable of perceiving this and accounting for it within their discursive matrices, the impetus remains on those of us who function, in however small a way, as gatekeepers and cultural mediators to shift our own modes of perception.

Bibliography

Achebe, Chinua, *No Longer at Ease* (London: Heinemann, 1960).

Arrow of God (London: Heinemann, 1964).

Hopes and Impediments: Selected Essays (New York: Anchor, 1988).

Things Fall Apart (New York: Anchor, 1994 [1958]).

Home and Exile (New York: Oxford University Press, 2000).

There Was A Country: A Personal History of Biafra (London: Allen Lane, 2012).

Adesokan, Akin, *Postcolonial Artists and Global Aesthetics* (Bloomington: Indiana University Press, 2011).

'"I'm Not An African Writer, Damn You!"', *Chronic Books Supplement*, December 2013, www.chimurengachronic.co.za/im-not-an-african-writer-damn-you/, accessed 29 January 2018.

Adichie, Chimamanda Ngozi, *Americanah* (London: Fourth Estate, 2013).

African Cities Reader, www.africancitiesreader.org.za/, accessed 29 January 2018.

Apter, Emily, *Against World Literature: On the Politics of Untranslatability* (London: Verso, 2013).

Bady, Aaron, 'The Varieties of Blackness: An Interview with Chimamanda Ngozi Adichie', *The Boston Review*, www.bostonreview.net/fiction/varieties-blackness, accessed 29 January 2018.

Balakrishnan, Sarah, 'Pan-African Legacies, Afropolitan Futures: A Conversation with Achille Mbembe', *Transition*, 120 (2016), 28–37.

Barber, Karin, (ed.), *Readings in African Popular Culture* (London: The International African Institute, 1997).

Bauman, Zygmunt, *Liquid Modernity* (Cambridge: Polity Press, 2012 [2000]).

Beautement, Tiah Marie, 'Editor's Note', *Tssf Journal*, 1 (2017), 3–4 (p. 3).

Beecroft, Alexander, *An Ecology of World Literature: From Antiquity to the Present Day* (London: Verso, 2014).

Benson, Peter, *Black Orpheus, Transition and Modern Cultural Awakening in Africa* (Berkeley: University of California Press, 1986).

Bond, Patrick, *Looting Africa: The Economics of Exploitation* (London: Zed Books, 2006).

Borman, David, 'Playful Ethnography: Chinua Achebe's Things Fall Apart and Nigerian Education', *ARIEL: A Review of International English Literature*, 46.3 (2015),91–112.

Bosch Santana, Stephanie, 'Exorcizing the Future: Afropolitanism's Spectral Origins', *Journal of African Cultural Studies*, 28.1 (2016), 120–6.

Brouillette, Sarah, *Postcolonial Writers in the Global Literary Marketplace* (Basingstoke: Palgrave Macmillan, 2005).

   'Neoliberalism and the Demise of the Literary', in *Neoliberalism and Contemporary Literary Culture*, ed. by Mitchum Huehls and Rachel Greenwald Smith (Baltimore: Johns Hopkins University Press, 2017), pp. 277–90.

   'On the African Literary Hustle', Blindfield Journal, 14 August 2017, www .blindfieldjournal.com/2017/08/14/on-the-african-literary-hustle/, accessed 31 January 2018.

Brown, Nicholas, *Utopian Generations: The Political Horizon of Twentieth-Century Literature* (Princeton: Princeton University Press, 2005).

Burgis, Tom, *The Looting Machine: Warlords, Tycoons, Smugglers and the Systematic Theft of Africa's Wealth* (London: HarperCollins, 2015).

Bush, Ruth, *Publishing Africa in French* (Liverpool: University of Liverpool Press, 2016).

Carmody, Pádraig, *The New Scramble for Africa* (Cambridge: Polity Press, 2011).

Carré, Nathalie, 'From Local to Global', *Wasafiri*, 31.4 (2016),56–62.

Casanova, Pascale, *The World Republic of Letters*, translated by Malcolm Debevoise (Cambridge: Harvard University Press, 2007).

Cheah, Pheng, *What is a World? On Postcolonial Literature as World Literature* (Durham: Duke University Press, 2016).

Chimurenga Chronic, 'About', www.chimurengachronic.co.za/about/, accessed 29 January 2018.

'*The Chronic*: New Cartographies March 2015', www.chimurenga.co.za/pro duct/the-chronic-new-cartographies-march-2015, accessed 29 January 2018.

Chimurenga Library, 'About', www.chimurengalibrary.co.za/about, accessed 29 January 2018.

Cobham Sanders, Rhonda, 'Problems of Gender and History in the Teaching of Things Fall Apart', in *Chinua Achebe's Things Fall Apart: A Casebook*, ed. by Isidore Okpewho (New York: Oxford University Press, 2003), pp. 165–80.

Cole, Teju, *Open City* (London: Faber and Faber, 2011).

'What It Is', *New Yorker*, 7 October 2014, www.newyorker.com/books/ page-turner/what-is-ebola, accessed 29 January 2018.

Cooper, Frederick, *Decolonization and African Society: The Labor Question in French and British Africa* (Cambridge: Cambridge University Press, 1996).

'Africa's Pasts and Africa's Historians', *Canadian Journal of African Studies / Revue Canadienne des Études Africaines*, 34.2 (2000), 298–336 (p. 300).

Currey, James, *Africa Writes Back: The African Writers Series and the Launch of African Literature* (Athens: Ohio University Press, 2008).

'Ngũgĩ, Leeds and the Establishment of African Literature', *Leeds African Studies Bulletin*, 74 (2012), 48–62 (pp. 48–9).

Currey, James and Randolph Vigne, *The New African: A History* (London: Merlin Press, 2014).

Dabiri, Emma, 'Why I Am (Still) Not An Afropolitan', *Journal of African Cultural Studies*, 28.1 (2016), 104–8.

Damrosch, David, *How to Read World Literature* (Oxford: Wiley & Blackwell, 2009).

Davis, Hassoldt, 'Jungle Strongman', *Saturday Review*, 31 January 1959, p. 18.

Day, Elizabeth, 'Americanah by Chimamanda Ngozi Adichie – review', *Guardian*, *15 April* 2013, www.theguardian.com/books/2013/apr/15/americanah-chimamanda-ngozi-adichie-review, accessed 29 January 2018.

Ducournau, Claire, *La fabrique des classiques africaines* (Paris: CNRS Éditions, 2017).

English, James, *The Economy of Prestige: Prizes, Awards, and the Circulation of Cultural Value* (Cambridge: Harvard University Press, 2005).

Eze, Chielozona, 'We, Afropolitans', *Journal of African Cultural Studies*, 28.1 (2016), 114–19.

Farafina Trust, www.farafinatrust.org/, accessed 29 January 2018.

Ferguson, James, *Global Shadows: Africa in the Neoliberal World Order* (Durham: Duke University Press, 2006).

Fraser, Robert, '"Who No Know Go Know": An Interview with Ntone Edjabe', *Wasafiri*, 22.3 (2007),62–67).

  Book History Through Postcolonial Eyes: Rewriting the Script (Abingdon: Routledge, 2008).

Gikandi, Simon, 'Chinua Achebe and the Invention of African Culture', *Research in African Literatures*, 32.3 (2001), 3–8.

Granqvist, Raoul, 'The Early Swedish Reviews of Chinua Achebe's Things Fall Apart and A Man of the People', *Research in African Literatures*, 15.3 (1984),394–404.

Habila, Helon, 'We Need New Names by NoViolet Bulawayo – Review', *Guardian*, 20 June 2013, www.theguardian.com/books/2013/jun/20/need-new-names-bulawayo-review, accessed 29 January 2018.

Haines, Kate, 'Q&A: Emmanuel Iduma – Writer and Co-Founder of *Saraba Magazine*', *Africa in Words*, 15 October 2015, www.africainwords

.com/2013/10/15/qa-emmanuel-iduma-writer-and-co-founder-of-sar aba-magazine/, accessed 29 January 2018.

Hammond, Dorothy and Alta Jablow, *The Africa that Never Was: Four Centuries of British Writing about Africa* (Prospect Heights, NY: Waveland Press, 1992).

Hardy, Stacy, 'A Brief History of Mapping', *The Chronic*, March 2015, p. 2.

Harvey, David, *Rebel Cities: From the Right to the City to the Urban Revolution* (London: Verso, 2012).

Huehls, Mitchum and Rachel Greenwald Smith, 'Four Phases of Neoliberalism and Literature: An Introduction', in *Neoliberalism and Contemporary Literary Culture*, ed. by Mitchum Huehls and Rachel Greenwald Smith (Baltimore: Johns Hopkins University Press, 2017), pp. 1–20.

Huggan, Graham, *The Postcolonial Exotic: Marketing the Margins* (London: Routledge, 2001).

Izevbaye, Dan, 'Chinua Achebe and the African Novel', in *The Cambridge Companion to the African Novel*, ed. by F. Abiola Irele (Cambridge: Cambridge University Press, 2009), pp. 31–50.

Jackson, Jeanne-Marie, 'New African Literature is Disrupting What Western Presses Prize', *The Conversation*, 9 October 2017, www.theconversation .com/new-african-literature-is-disrupting-what-western-presses-prize-85206, accessed 29 March 2018.

Jameson, Fredric, *Postmodernism, or, the Cultural Logic of Late Capitalism* (Durham: Duke University Press, 1991).

Julien, Eileen, 'The Extroverted African Novel', in *The Novel: History, Geography and Culture. Vol 1*, ed. Franco Moretti (Princeton: Princeton University Press, 2006), pp. 667–700.

Kiguru, Doseline, 'Literary Prizes, Writers' Organisations and Canon Formation in Africa', *African Studies*, 75.2 (2016), 202–14.

'Prizing African Literature: Creating a Literary Taste', *Social Dynamics*, 42.1 (2016), 161–74.

Knudsen, Eva Rask and Ulla Rahbek, *In Search of the Afropolitan* (London: Rowman and Littlefield, 2016).

Krishnan, Madhu, *Contemporary African Literature in English: Global Locations, Postcolonial Identifications* (Basingstoke: Palgrave Macmillan, 2014).

'Postcoloniality, Spatiality and Cosmopolitanism in the Open City', *Textual Practice*, 29.4 (2015), 675–96.

'From Empire to Independence: Colonial Space in the Writing of Tutuola, Ekwensi, Beti, and Kane', *Comparative Literature Studies*, 54.2 (2017), 329–57.

'Periodizing the Anglophone African Novel: Location(s) in a Transnational Literary Marketplace', in *Literature and the Global Contemporary*, ed. by Sarah Brouillette, Mathias Nilges, and Emilio Sauri (Basingstoke: Palgrave Macmillan, 2017), pp. 135–56.

Kwani Trust, 'Bookstores', www.kwani.org/publications/book-store.htm, accessed 29 January 2018.

'Our History', www.kwani.org/our-history/kwani.htm, accessed 29 January 2018.

Laye, Camara, *L'enfant noir* (Paris: Librairie Plon, 1953).

MacViban, Dzekashu, 'Q & A with Ntone Edjabe on Chimurenga, Fela, and Politics', *Bakwa Magazine*, 18 August 2012, www.bakwamagazine.com/2012/08/18/conversation-ntone-edjabe-by-breaking-the-divide-between-the-public-and-the-private-he-fela-expanded-our-vocabulary-of-resistance-the-musician-was-no-longer-simply-an-entertainer/, accessed 29 January 2018.

Marechera, Dambudzo, *The House of Hunger* (London: Heinemann Educational Books, 2009 [1978]).

Marzagora, Sara, 'African-Language Literatures and the "Transnational Turn" in Euro-American Humanities', *Journal of African Cultural Studies*, 27.1 (2015), 40–55.

Maslin, Janet, 'Braiding Hair and Issues About Race', *New York Times*, 19 May 2013, www.nytimes.com/2013/05/20/books/americanha-by-chimamanda-ngozi-adichie.html, accessed 29 January 2018.

Massey, Doreen, *Space, Place and Gender* (Cambridge: Polity Press, 1994).

Mbembe, Achille, 'At the Centre of the Knot', *Social Dynamics*, 38.1 (2012),8–14.

    Critique de la raison nègre (Paris: La Découverte, 2013).

    A Critique of Black Reason, translated by Laurent Dubois (Durham: Duke University Press, 2017).

Mbue, Imbolo, *Behold the Dreamers* (London: Fourth Estate, 2016).

McDonald, Peter D., 'Instituting (World) Literature', in *Institutions of World Literature: Writing, Translation, Markets*, ed. by Stefan Helgesson and Pieter Vermeulen (London: Routledge, 2015), pp. 39–52 (pp. 39–42).

McDonald, Robert, 'Bound to Violence: A Case of Plagiarism', *Transition*, 41 (1972), 64–8.

Musila, Grace A., 'Part-Time Africans, Europolitans and "Africa lite"', *Journal of African Cultural Studies*, 28.1 (2016), 109–13.

Ndebele, Njabulo, 'Thinking of Brenda', *Chimurenga 1: Music is the Weapon*, (2002),pp. ; 1–6.

Ndjio, Basile, 'Carrefour de la joie: Popular Deconstruction of the African Postcolonial Public Sphere', *Africa: Journal of the International African Institute*, 74.3 (2005), 265–94.

Nesbitt-Ahmed, Zahrah, 'Reclaiming African Literature in The Digital Age: An Exploration of Online Literary Platforms', *Critical African Studies*, 9.3 (2017), 377–90.

Newell, Stephanie, *West African Literature: Ways of Reading* (Oxford: Oxford University Press, 2006).

Ochiagha, Terri, *Achebe and Friends at Umuahia: The Making of a Literary Elite* (Oxford: James Currey, 2015).

Ogbe, Yemisi, 'Americanah and Other Definitions of Supple Citizenship', *Chronic Books Supplement*, August 2013, pp. 8–11 (p. 10).

Olney, James, 'The African Novel in Transition: Chinua Achebe', *South Atlantic Quarterly*, 70 (1971), 299–316.

Pan African Space Station, www.panafricanspacestation.org.za/, accessed 29 January 2018.

Peed, Mike, 'Realities of Race', *New York Times*, 7 June 2013, www.nytimes.com/2013/06/09/books/review/americanah-by-chimamanda-ngozi-adichie.html, accessed 29 January 2018.

Peterson, Derek R., Emma Hunter, and Stephanie Newell (eds), *African Print Cultures: Newspapers and Their Publics in the Twentieth Century* (Ann Arbor: University of Michigan Press, 2016).

Quayson, Ato, *Calibrations: Reading for the Social* (Minneapolis: University of Minnesota Press, 2003).

  Oxford Street, Accra: City Life and the Itineraries of Transnationalism (Durham: Duke University Press, 2014).

Rawson, Philip Stanley, 'The Centre Cannot Hold', *Times Literary Supplement* 20 June 1958, p. 341.

Rodman, Selden, 'The White Man's Faith', *New York Times Book Review* 22 February 1959, p. 28.

Rosen, Zachary, 'Abdi Latif Ega and the Rejection of The "African" Novel', *Africa is a Country*, 24 February 2016, www.africasacountry.com/2016/02/abdi-latif-ega-and-the-rejection-of-the-african-novel/, accessed 29 January 2018.

Segoete, Lineo, 'Ba re e ne re: Building a Community of Writers and Readers in Lesotho', *Africa in Words*, 23 May 2017, www.africainwords.com/2017/05/22/ba-re-e-ne-re-building-a-community-of-writers-and-readers-in-lesotho/, accessed 29 January 2018.

Selasi, Taiye, 'Bye-Bye Babar', *The LIP Magazine*, 3 March 2005, www.thelip .robertsharp.co.uk/?p=76, accessed 29 January 2018.

Sellin, Eric, 'Ouologuem's Blueprint for *Le devoir de violence*', *Research in African Literatures*, 2.2 (1971), 117.

Shercliff, Emma, 'The Valentine's Day Anthology: A Snapshot of the Possibilities and Challenges of African Publishing', *Africa in Words*, 5 March 2015, www .africainwords.com/2015/03/05/the-valentines-day-anthology-a-snap shot-of-the-possibilities-and-challenges-of-african-publishing/, accessed 29 January 2018.

   'African Publishing in the Twenty-First Century', *Wasafiri*, 31.4 (2016), 10–12.

Smit, Sara, 'Finding Affiliations: Reading Communities, Literary Institutions & Small Magazines', *Africa in Words*, 21 October 2017, www .africainwords.com/2017/10/21/finding-affiliations-reading-communities-literary-institutions-small-magazines/, accessed 29 January 2018.

Snyder, Carey, 'The Possibilities and Pitfalls of Ethnographic Readings: Narrative Complexity in Things Fall Apart', *College Literature*, 35.2 (2008), 154–75.

Spence, Lester K., *Knocking the Hustle: Against the Neoliberal Turn in Black Politics* (New York: Punctum Books, 2016).

Stauhs, Doreen, *African Literary NGOs: Power, Politics and Participation* (Basingstoke: Palgrave Macmillan, 2013).

Suhr-Sytsma, Nathan, 'A Secret History of the Nation': Small Magazines at Writivism 2017', *Africa in Words*, www.africainwords.com/2017/10/30/

a-secret-history-of-the-nation-small-magazines-at-writivism-2017/, accessed 29 January 2018.

'The Extroverted African Novel and Literary Publishing in the Twenty-First Century', Journal of African Cultural Studies, 9 November 2017, doi: 10.1080/13696815.2017.1400953,www.tandfonline.com/doi/abs/10.1080/13696815.2017.1400953, accessed 29 January 2018.

Taylor, Ian, *Africa Rising? BRICS – Diversifying Dependency* (Woodbridge: Boydell & Brewer, 2014).

The Caine Prize for African Writing, 'About Us', www.caineprize.com/about/, accessed 29 January 2018.

Toivanen, Anna-Leena, 'Cosmopolitanism's New Clothes? The Limits of the Concept of Afropolitanism', *European Journal of English Studies*, 21.2 (2017), 189–205.

wa Ngũgĩ, Mũkoma and Laura T. Murphy, 'Introducing Issue 43: This Hustle Is Not Your Grandpa's African Lit', *New Orleans Review*, 43 (2017), www.neworleansreview.org/this-hustle-is-not-your-grandpas-african-lit/, accessed 29 January 2018.

wa Ngũgĩ, Mũkoma, *The Rise of the African Novel: Politics of Language, Identity and Ownership* (Ann Arbor: University of Michigan Press, 2018).

wa Thiong'o, Ngũgĩ, 'On the Abolition of the English Department', in *The Post-colonial Studies Reader*, ed. by Bill Ashcroft, Gareth Griffiths and Helen Tiffin (New York: Routledge, 1995), pp. 438–42.

Wallis, Kate, 'How Books Matter: Kwani Trust, Farafina, Cassava Republic and the Medium of Print', *Wasafiri*, 31.4 (2016), 39–46.

'Exchanges in Nairobi and Lagos: Literary Networks as Alternative Geographies', *Research in African Literatures*, 49.1 (2018), 163–186.

Wanberg, Kyle, 'Ghostwriting History: Subverting the Reception of Le regard du roi and *Le devoir de violence*', *Comparative Literature Studies*, 50.4 (2013), 598–617.

Warwick Research Collective, (WReC), *Combined and Uneven Development: Towards a New Theory of World-Literature* (Liverpool: University of Liverpool Press, 2015).

Wawrzinek, Jennifer and J. K. S. Makokha (eds), *Negotiating Afropolitanism: Essays on Borders and Spaces in Contemporary African Literature and Folklore* (Amsterdam: Rodopi, 2011).

Wilson-Tagoe, Nana, 'Literary Prizes and the Creation of Literary Culture: Judging African Literature in Pan-Commonwealth and Pan-African Competitions', *Wasafiri*, 20.46 (2005), 58–61.

Zell, Hans, 'Publishing in Africa', in *International Book Publishing: An Encyclopedia*. ed. by P. G. Altbach and E. S. Hoshino (New York: Garland Publishing, 1995), pp. ;366–73.

Cambridge Elements

Publishing and Book Culture

Series Editor
Samantha Rayner
University College London

Samantha Rayner is a Reader in UCL's Department of Information Studies. She is also Director of UCL's Centre for Publishing, co-Director of the Bloomsbury CHAPTER (Communication History, Authorship, Publishing, Textual Editing and Reading) and co-editor of the Academic Book of the Future BOOC (Book as Open Online Content) with UCL Press.

Associate Editor
Rebecca Lyons
University of Bristol

Rebecca Lyons is a Teaching Fellow at the University of Bristol. She is also co-editor of the experimental BOOC (Book as Open Online Content) at UCL Press. She teaches and researches book and reading history, particularly female owners and readers of Arthurian literature in fifteenth- and sixteenth-century England, and also has research interests in digital academic publishing.

Advisory Board

About the series

This series aims to fill the demand for easily accessible, quality texts
available for teaching and research in the diverse and dynamic fields of
Publishing and Book Culture. Rigorously researched and peer-reviewed
Elements will be published under themes, or 'Gatherings'. These Elements
should be the first check point for researchers or students working on that
area of publishing and book trade history and practice: we hope that,
situated so logically at Cambridge University Press, where academic
publishing in the UK began, it will develop to create an unrivalled space
where these histories and practices can be investigated and preserved.

Cambridge Elements

Publishing and Book Culture
Publishing the Canon

Gathering Editor:
Leah Tether

Leah Tether is a Reader in Medieval Literature and Digital Cultures at the University of Bristol. Her research is on historical publishing practices from manuscript to digital, and she has a special interest in Arthurian literature of the Middle Ages. She is the author of *Publishing the Grail in Medieval and Renaissance France* (D. S. Brewer, 2017).

ELEMENTS IN THE GATHERING

A full series listing is available at: www.cambridge.org/EPBC

Printed in the United States
By Bookmasters